LIVE A PRAYING LIFE® IN ADVERSITY

JENNIFER KENNEDY DEAN

LIVE A PRAYING LIFE® IN ADVERSITY

WHY YOU KEEP PRAYING WHEN YOU WANT TO GIVE UP

NEW HOPE
PUBLISHERS
Gospel-Centered. Missions-Driven.

BIRMINGHAM, ALABAMA

New Hope® Publishers
PO Box 12065
Birmingham, AL 35202-2065
NewHopeDigital.com
New Hope Publishers is a division of WMU®.

Library of Congress Control Number: 2014943193

Unless otherwise indicated, Scripture quotations marked NIV are taken from THE HOLY BIBLE, NEW INTERNATIONAL VERSION®, NIV® Copyright © 1973, 1978, 1984, 2011 by Biblica, Inc.® Used by permission. All rights reserved worldwide.

Scripture quotation marked NIV 1984 is taken from THE HOLY BIBLE, NEW INTERNATIONAL VERSION®, NIV® Copyright © 1973, 1978, 1984 by Biblica, Inc.® Used by permission. All rights reserved worldwide.

Scripture quotations marked AMP are taken from the Amplified® Bible, Copyright © 1954, 1958, 1962, 1964, 1965, 1987 by The Lockman Foundation. Used by permission.

Scripture quotations marked ESV are from The Holy Bible, English Standard Version, copyright © 2001 by Crossway Bibles, a division of Good News Publishers. Used by permission. All rights reserved.

Scripture quotations marked KJV are taken from The Holy Bible, King James Version.

Scripture quotations marked NASB are taken from the New American Standard Bible®, Copyright © 1960, 1962, 1963, 1968, 1971, 1972, 1973, 1975, 1977, 1995 by The Lockman Foundation. Used by permission.

Scripture quotations marked *The Message* are taken from *The Message* by Eugene H. Peterson. Copyright © 1993, 1994, 1995, 1996, 2000, 2001, 2002. Used by permission of NavPress Publishing Group.

Quotation on page 22 used by permission. R. Jamieson, A. R. Fausset, and D. Brown, *Commentary Critical and Explanatory on the Whole Bible* (Oak Harbor, WA: Logos Research Systems, Inc.), 1997.

ISBN-10: 1-59669-410-6
ISBN-13: 978-1-59669-410-1
N144116 • 0814 • 4M1

DEDICATION

Brantley and Caroline

Kennedy and Sara

Stinson and Stephanie

I'm so proud of the wonderful adults you have become.

CONTENTS

SPECIAL INTERACTIVE VIDEOS FEATURED IN THIS CONTENT.

See and use these QR codes that you will find
in each chapter throughout this content.
You will see and hear Jennifer Kennedy Dean
sharing about *Live a Praying Life® in Adversity.*

For more information on New Hope QR codes, please go to
NewHopeDigital.com/QR.

To find additional *Live a Praying Life®* resources by Jennifer,
please go to NewHopeDigital.com.

INTRODUCTION

The concept of a praying life has informed my life and shaped my message for as long as I have been pursuing a present-tense relationship with the living, indwelling Jesus. From the time He first got a firm grip on my heart, prayer has been my pursuit. *Live a Praying Life*® is the culmination of how the Lord has taught me and answered my heart's cry. I think of *Live a Praying Life* as the purpose for which I was born. It is my passion and my driving force.

If the truths laid out in *Live a Praying Life* are genuine, then they work when life is at its worst. When my husband passed away in 2005, I was often asked if the experience changed anything I believed about prayer. My answer is no. It confirmed what I had learned over my lifetime about prayer.

Truths about prayer have never shown up in my life simply as theory. Rather, each truth was road tested as it was built into my life and forged in the heat of real life experience.

This study takes the principles of *Live a Praying Life* and applies them directly to times of adversity. Either they work in the realities of living life — or they are untrue. They can't remain a hypothesis. They have to be put to the test in the faith lab of life and proven to be solid and dependable.

My go-to verse is Jeremiah 33:3. This is what fascinates me over and over. "Call to me and I will answer you and *tell you great and unsearchable things you do not know*" (author's emphasis). In the course of a praying life, God reveals more and more of Himself. His answer to our call includes revelation and insight and new ways to see old truths. He makes direct deposits from His heart into ours, and we change. We change our outlook, our ideas, our understanding. All because we called to Him and He answered us with truths we did not know before we called.

If you have read my book *Fueled by Faith,* you will recognize the principles I expand and apply to how to live a praying life in adversity.

WEEK 1

THE PURPOSE OF PRAYER

The purpose of prayer is to release the power of God to accomplish the purposes of God. The purpose of prayer is to discover God's will, not obligate Him to do mine; to reflect God's mind, not change it.

Prayer is the means by which you will be freed from your earthbound, timebound thinking to participate in eternity. True prayer releases His power so that His power can accomplish immeasurably more than we can ask or even imagine (see Ephesians 3:20).

— Live a Praying Life®: Open Your Life to God's Power and Provision

DAY 1

Life has adversity. We have to come to terms with the fact that there is no escaping it. Perhaps the reason you picked up this book is because you are currently experiencing adversity of some kind.

Let's define *adversity*: hardship, distress, difficulty, affliction, misfortune. For our purposes, let me impose some parameters. Adversity is something in your life that you view as negative and that you can't change or fix. Every single person I know has something in his or her life that fits that definition. I know famous, platform-speaking, book-writing people, and I know people who live their lives privately. I know rich people and I know people who struggle to make ends meet. I know people who seem to have everything they could dream of, and I know people who seem to lose at every turn. I don't know one person who does not have adversity in life—something he or she desperately wishes would change. Often, the experience of our adversity forms the content of our prayers. Asking for relief. Looking for escape. Hoping for deliverance.

It is adversity that first brings many to prayer. And it is adversity that drives many from faith. Difficulties and disappointments will come. You can count on it. No one escapes. This is so sure a reality that Jesus states it clearly. "In this world, you will have trouble" (John 16:33). The question is not, "Will I experience adversity?" but rather, "Will I allow adversity to break me or to build me?"

Clearly define the adverse situation(s) with which you are currently struggling. What do you want God to change or correct? Be specific as you write this out and establish clearly in your mind the contours of your current struggle.

PRAYER'S PURPOSE

Perhaps in your experience of adversity, and the prayers it has prompted, you feel that prayer is not getting through or making any difference. Maybe you are just about to conclude that prayer is of no use, or that God doesn't get involved in the details of your life, or that you are not worthy of His grace and help in time of need.

Maybe you have been feverishly searching for the method or the formula that will get God to act. Possibly you have been trying hard to come up with enough faith to satisfy God and convince Him to do what you feel needs to be done. All to no avail. It seems heaven is closed to you. Surely there is some secret to getting God to act, but you don't know what it is.

Let's start here. Prayer is not a magic formula that turns God into a genie who makes your wish His command. You will not find a secret formula for prayer that gives you the power to get your will accomplished in every situation. So, then, what does prayer do?

Prayer is the conduit through which God's power and provision flow from the heavenly realms to the circumstances of earth. It is not our role to decide what God should do and then talk Him into doing it. Prayer opens your life to the flow of His power and provision. Prayer is not a tool for getting God to carry out your wishes or to follow your instructions. Instead, prayer releases the power of God for the purposes of God.

God has not made prayer tricky, so that only a few can get it right. He has made it simple and accessible because it is His strategy for bringing the power of heaven into the environment of earth.

Could it be that prayer is so simple that any child of God can lay hold of all God's power and provision through His designated strategy called *prayer*? It is the most powerful weapon in our spiritual arsenal, and He has designed it to work, and to be a weapon that can be wielded by anyone in whom Christ resides through faith.

Decades ago God began to redefine prayer for me. I came to understand it as a continual interaction between the spiritual realm and the material realm—an unceasing flow from His heart to mine. I quit thinking about how to say prayers and began to live a praying life.

I learned that every thought can be instantly turned in God's direction and so become prayer. I learned that the Holy Spirit can make direct deposits from His heart to mine and awaken thoughts and desires that become the content of my praying. In these years of learning how to live a praying life, I have come to realize that if God designed prayer to work, not to fail, then He surely designed it to be accessible and simple.

I think we see this pictured clearly in a story John records. He tells the story of a wedding at which Jesus was a guest and His mother seemed to be in charge behind the scenes. (See John 2.)

When the wine ran out, apparently the servants turned to Mary with their problem. I'm imagining the scene when a servant came running to Mary, concern apparent in his demeanor and his inflections. "Mary! They have no wine!" He puts the whole burden on her. Their wineless state has now become her responsibility. She has to come through.

I think she says something like, "Don't worry. I've got it covered."

She turns to Jesus and says, "Jesus, they have no wine." (See v. 3.)

He makes a response to her that our twenty-first-century, perhaps Gentile, ears hear as a rebuke. But let's hear it again: "Woman!" He says. A word of endearment. The same word He used from the Cross to say, "Woman, behold your son." Addressing her gently. Then He uses a Hebrew idiom that His contemporaries would have heard as (my paraphrase), "Now that has nothing to do with you and everything to do with Me." The Amplified Bible translates it like this: "What do we have in common? Leave it to Me" (v. 4 AMP).

Then He said that His time had not yet come. Did He violate His sense of timing to please or appease His mother? No. He was warning her that the time to reveal His actions publicly had not come. She had to let someone else get all the credit for what her son had done.

The master of the banquet tasted the water that had been turned into wine. He did not realize where it had come from, though the servants who had drawn the water knew. Then he called the bridegroom aside and said, "Everyone brings out the choice wine first and then the cheaper wine after the guests have had too much to drink; but you have saved the best till now" (vv. 9–10).

Notice that the response did not deter Mary. She didn't slink away as if scolded. She turned to the servants and said, "Do whatever he tells you" (v. 5). She knew Jesus, so she knew there would be action. She didn't know what that action would look like, but she had learned that Jesus would know what to do.

I can't imagine that she expected a miracle. Why would she? He had never performed a miracle before. "What Jesus did here in Cana of Galilee was the first of the signs through which he revealed his glory" (v. 11). She didn't know *what* He would do, but she knew *that* He would do.

Do you see how simple her request was? She didn't feel compelled to tell Him what to do and how to do it. She didn't have to beg, plead, or cajole. She knew that when she took the burden that sat on her shoulders and handed it over to Jesus, He would know what to do and how to do it. She knew that the secret to powerful praying is to take God the need, not the answer.

Sometimes the most powerful prayer sounds something like this: "Jesus, they have no wine."

Are there times when you feel responsible for coming up with the answer for God? What is burdening your heart right now? What is your "they have no wine" prayer?

ADVERSITY'S WORK

Consider it pure joy, my brothers and sisters, whenever you face trials of many kinds, because you know that the testing of your faith produces perseverance. Let perseverance finish its work so that you may be mature and complete, not lacking anything (James 1:2–4).

God has no purpose in your life but good. His will is "good, pleasing, and perfect" (Romans 12:2). His plans are for your good, for your benefit, for your ultimate happiness and fulfillment. He is not devising scenarios for your failure, or creating circumstances to test your burden-bearing prowess.

Have you heard it said, "God will not give you more than you can bear"? Not exactly an untrue statement, but it implies something untrue about God. It implies that He is piling burdens on you so that He can test your mettle. He is not the great burden giver, but instead He is the great burden bearer. He will indeed give you — or allow into your life — more than you can bear and will use those circumstances to help you learn how to transfer burdens to Him.

"We were under great pressure, far beyond our ability to endure, so that we despaired even of life. Indeed, we felt we had received the sentence of death. But this happened that we might not rely on ourselves but on God, who raises the dead" (2 Corinthians 1:8–9; author's emphasis).

—〰—

More Than You Can Bear: Adversity That Redefines Joy
Let Teri Bledsoe tell her story:

Hello, my name is Teri Bledsoe, and I am a recovering joy addict.

I know I'm playing the blame game here, but I attribute this addiction to my theology, or rather the misguided theology I used to embrace. I thought if I could just please God by keeping my sin to the minimum, I'd be happy. The way I saw it, joyful circumstances were evidence of God's favor. And the converse was true. If I experienced loss, adversity, or pain, to me it was a sure bet that God was punishing me. So it makes perfect sense that I used to avoid suffering at all costs. Who wouldn't?

And then my real life happened, with all the glorious ups and downs of any real life. First, the struggle of infertility and then the blessing of adoption. Next, the anguish of mental illness in two of our four children. Enough hard things to make joy seem like an impossibility, even to me.

Impossibility: the first step to addiction recovery. The thing is, joy is possible, but only in the proper context, in the presence of God. Over the past 15 years, the Holy Spirit tenderly and lovingly met me in my "impossible" circumstances and taught me that adversity is an invitation to journey toward joy: "You make known to me the path of life; in Your presence there is fullness of joy; at Your right hand are pleasures forevermore" (Psalm 16:11 ESV). With God, joy is found in His presence, not at the end of the path, but on and in the midst of it. Along the way, I've learned to

- *lock my mind on the things I know to be true about God's love for me through Jesus Christ;*
- *fix my eyes on Jesus (Hebrews 12:2) by turning over and trusting the situation to His loving care;*
- *thank God that whatever the circumstance, it is the most loving thing He could allow for me in that moment;*
- *watch and wait for God to reveal His presence and provision to me; and*
- *obediently do whatever the Holy Spirit seems to be urging me to do next — one step at a time.*

This does not mean I began to enjoy adversity. But now, I see it through God's eyes. He has anointed my suffering as an opportunity to manifest His presence, His character and His glory to me and through me. I often refer to raising children with mental illness as walking through the wilderness. At times, I have found the wilderness to be dark and scary, lonely and barren, and more than I can do emotionally and physically. Yet, the Holy Spirit has guided the eyes of my heart to seek and find grace in the wilderness (Jeremiah 31:2), and the hidden gifts of adversity — His joy, comfort, strength, and peace.

—⟊—

GOD IS NOT PUNISHING YOU

As you process this adversity in your life, first know that it is not a punishment. It is not God trying to find your limits. Some adversity is indeed the result of sinful choices. But it is not punishment. If it were punishment, then the Cross didn't quite get the job done. Hold that thought. We'll come back to it.

Let's talk about consequences of sinful choices. Do you get the full consequence of every sinful choice you make? You certainly don't, or you would not be alive right now. After all, "the wages of sin is death" (Romans 6:23). The Father has filtered the consequences so that only those that will lead you to repentance and will be His opening for restoration will reach you. Does sin have consequences? Yes, it does. Do you reap those consequences in full measure? You do not.

Sometimes your adversity is the consequence of someone else's choices. You feel like the victim, left to clean up someone else's mess. The same truth holds. God has filtered what touches you. It has been carefully thought out with your benefit in mind. God doesn't have a one-track mind. He can have His full attention on every layer, every nuance, every individual that makes up a circumstance. He is working out good and beneficial results at every stratum of the event. No one is left out of His loving activity. Nothing is left to chance. You are never a helpless victim of another's choices, though it may appear so at the time.

Think of Joseph, who seemed to be the victim of his evil brothers' whims and decisions, but instead was being moved by God's hand into the very place where the promise of God would materialize.

DAY 2

TESTING OF YOUR FAITH

James 1:3 uses the phrase "testing of your faith." Let's delve into that some. God deposited faith in you at your salvation. He did not leave it up to you to see if you could come up with faith.

Underline or highlight the phrases or words in the following Scripture quotations that tell you that your faith came to you as a gift from God. Then respond to the questions.

"It is Jesus' name and the faith that comes through him that has completely healed him, as you can all see" (Acts 3:16).

"For by the grace given me I say to every one of you: Do not think of yourself more highly than you ought, but rather think of yourself with sober judgment, in accordance with the faith God has distributed to each of you" (Romans 12:3).

"For it is by grace you have been saved, through faith — and this not from yourselves, it is the gift of God" (Ephesians 2:8). If God put faith on deposit, does He know how much faith you have?

Would He need to devise tests to see the quality or quantity of your faith, since it came from Him?

Would it benefit you if you learned about the quality of the faith God has deposited in you?

Is God testing your faith so He can see its quality, or so that you can see its quality?

If your faith is never used, will you know about the amazing gift God has given you?

The testing of your faith does not suggest a difficulty devised by God so He can see if you measure up. Instead, He is using your current situation positively in your life, proving to you that you have the faith that will bring you the victory in due time. You are not at the mercy of your circumstances. The better translation for the Greek word *dokimion* (translated "test," as in James 1:3) might be "prove." It means to prove something to be genuine, or up to the task. The proof is for you. God already knows. According to *Commentary Critical and Explanatory on the Whole Bible,* "Every possible trial to the child of God is a masterpiece of strategy of the Captain of his salvation for his good."

Your current adversity is not punishment, and neither is it a test you have to pass. Proven faith will allow you to live with confidence that you are fully supplied for everything life brings. Tested, proven faith is of more value to you than gold.

In all this you greatly rejoice, though now for a little while you may have had to suffer grief in all kinds of trials. These have come so that the proven genuineness of your faith — of greater worth than gold, which perishes even though refined by fire — may result in praise, glory and honor when Jesus Christ is revealed (1 Peter 1:6–7).

God deposited faith in you because He knew you would need it. He has given you enough faith. He hasn't given you just enough to scrape by. He has lavished His gift on you. You have enough faith to come out the victor because God doesn't skimp on His gifts. You will be richer and better because of the adversity you are walking through. It will not diminish you. It will build you.

DIVE INTO THE DEEP END

To understand the purpose of prayer in the midst of adversity, you have to wrestle with a few questions and come to a solid understanding of God's design for life that allows for adversity to be part of the picture — from petty annoyances to excruciating grief. Let's tackle it head on.

Do you have enough faith? If you are like most Christians, your answer is no. Maybe you say it with shame, feeling that if you were more spiritual or a better Christian, you would have "enough faith." Maybe you say it piously, thinking that no one could possibly have "enough faith." Maybe you think it would be unseemly and arrogant to answer yes.

Don't edit yourself or try to figure out the right answer. There is no right answer. Just respond honestly. Do you have enough faith?

Why did you answer as you did?

What experiences or beliefs have convinced you that you either do or do not have enough faith?

I'm going to make some guesses. I'm going to guess that many of you answered no to the question, "Do you have enough faith?" Somewhere along the line, your faith has taken a hit from which you have not recovered. Maybe you explained it something like this: "I had faith that God would heal my son, but he died. I must not have had enough faith." Or maybe your story goes like this: "I had faith that God would restore my marriage, but my husband went through with the divorce. I feel that God let me down. Now I can't make myself believe that I can trust Him for anything." My own journey to understand prayer and the faith that lays prayer's foundation began with just such an experience.

MY FAITH PASSAGE

The summer following my graduation from high school, my only brother, who was two years my junior and my best friend, was diagnosed with a rare and deadly form of leukemia. Because of my mother's strong prayer network and my parents' absolute faith in God, Roger's illness was covered in prayer continually. We firmly believed that his body would be restored, and even when his symptoms worsened that belief did not waver. Throughout the year of his illness, we saw many instances of healing—times when the doctors gave up hope, or when a new and serious symptom would emerge. When he was first diagnosed, the immediate life-threatening danger was a large cantaloupe-sized tumor that was crushing his bronchial tubes, making difficult for him to breathe, and had pushed his organs out of place so that his heart was beside his stomach. It was already at such a stage that Roger's death could be only days away. Our church opened its doors to the community for prayer and word is that a standing-room-only crowd attended. Our family was at the hospital 100 miles away, but many who were present report that there was a discernable, almost physical, sense of the Lord's presence. By the next morning, the tumor had shrunk by half. A week later it was gone entirely. Time and time again, miraculous healing of symptoms occurred and it affirmed our faith. Yet, a year after his disease had been diagnosed, my sweet brother died, the withered shell of his body lying in a hospital bed.

As sick as he was, the news of his death was the last thing I expected to hear. Yet, at that moment, what I can only describe as a blanket of peace covered me. My family members all report the same experience. I did not know the Lord and His ways well at that time. But I did not have to do or believe anything to receive His love that literally overpowered what the responses of my flesh would have been. His intervention in every detail of the situation continued to be obvious as He comforted us in supernatural ways.

Later, left-brain analytical thinker that God has created me to be, I began to wonder, *If all that prayer for his healing was going on, and Roger died anyway, what good was prayer?* It compelled me into a search for answers and understanding that has defined the call of God on my life. God produced something eternal through Roger's death. His life was a seed that fell into the ground to produce a harvest.

EXPLAINING AWAY

You will hear many unsatisfying answers to the questions about faith that such an experience births. Someone will be sure to say, "You didn't have enough faith." You might search your memory for moments of uncertainty and doubt and, to your shame, recall just such feelings along the way. Since then, you have been saddled with the terrible burden of feeling that if only you could have had enough faith, things would have turned out differently. You find yourself afraid to exercise faith, knowing that you failed at faith just when your faith was most necessary.

Another explanation you are sure to hear is, "People have free will. God doesn't force anyone. We live in an evil world and sometimes evil wins." If you accept that theory, you develop a theology that says sometimes God is helpless in the face of determined evil. Your understanding of God is that He is free will's victim and sometimes slinks away in defeat. How can you really trust that God? Aren't the outcomes of most circumstances contingent upon some human's freely made decision? So wouldn't God be thwarted more times than not?

Think about an event that shakes your faith. Maybe something that happened to you, or to someone you know, or the tragedies of every description that we see on the nightly news. Think about the infamous day of September 11, 2001. Think of something specific that makes you wonder where a God who claims to be both good and all-powerful was at that moment. Think specifically as we wrestle this out.

Where was God at that moment? Was He helpless? Was there a different outcome that He tried His best to accomplish, but He just fell short? Was He outmaneuvered by the enemy? Was He thwarted by man's free will and evil intentions?

FAITH THAT REASONS

Faith is the highest form of reasoning. I know you have heard that faith and reason are polar opposites. Not so. Faith is logic in its purest form because faith is locked on to the reality of eternity. True logic and reason are God's gifts to us, but they only work if they are based on reality, not speculation. Faith is being sure of what you cannot see, but just because your eyes cannot see it does not mean it is not real. What you cannot see — the spiritual realities — are the firm and unshakable realities of life. I am going to challenge you right now to reason, letting your faith enlighten your intellect. Faith can allow for the worst-case scenario and still be fearless. Why? Because God is in charge.

Do you recall the faith of Shadrach, Meshach, and Abednego recorded in Daniel 3:17–18?

If we are thrown into the blazing furnace, the God we serve is able to save us from it, and he will deliver us from Your Majesty's hand. But even if he does not, we want you to know, Your Majesty, that we will not serve your gods or worship the image of gold you have set up.

They knew that even if the worst possible scenario occurred, God was being faithful. They did not know whether or not they would be thrown into the fire. They did not say, "I'm believing for God to keep me from the fiery furnace." They said, "We trust God, no matter the outcome."

King Nebuchadnezzar, the king of Babylon where the three young men were captives, had declared an image he had created to be God and had made a law that anyone who did not bow down to that image would be thrown into a fiery furnace. Shadrach, Meshach, and Abednego knew that they would never obey the king's edict. They would never worship Nebuchadnezzar's idol. They also knew that meant that they would face a situation intended to bring a sure and horrific death. They had their confidence so focused on God that they knew that He could keep them from facing the fiery furnace, but that if He did not, it would still have a good outcome. Not only did they not escape the king's punishment, but the fire was heated up seven times hotter than usual. They got the worst of the worst.

Let's pursue the argument to its conclusion. Part of this whole line of reasoning is that if it is good, then God did it and if it is bad, then God had nothing to do with it. "Don't go blaming God," someone will say. "After all, we live in a fallen world, and evil happens." I have a couple of problems with the logic of that position. First, you can't believe half a thought. Do you believe that God sometimes stops evil or bad things from happening? Or do you believe that evil always has its way and operates without interference from God? I think you will say that God sometimes stops evil and overrules disaster. That's the first half of the thought and I believe it is true. God sometimes intervenes to stop difficulties and disasters. The rest of the thought is this: if He sometimes intervenes to stop bad things from happening, then when He does not stop them, He does not stop them on purpose. Otherwise, when He does not stop bad things from happening, then is He careless? Distracted? Powerless? Can He tell you to trust Him and rest in Him because He is in charge . . . unless, of course, someone wants to use his or her free will or unless your enemy devises an evil plan against you? Under those circumstances, He is out of the picture. Both halves of the thought have to fit. One part of the thought can't nullify the other.

Take the next logical step in reasoning out this truth. God is only good. No evil or negative purpose dwells in His heart. He can divert any difficulty or disaster, big or little, and He most often does so. When He does not — when He purposefully allows a difficulty, a challenge, a heartache, a disaster — His purposes are good and loving.

I have had many a person say to me when I discuss this thought, "Well, I can't see any good that could come out of — " and then they go on to describe a terrible and tragic situation. I need to challenge you, then, if this is what you are thinking. Is that the measure? Is that the deciding factor? Whether or not you can see? Whether you can perceive?

Faith is knowing that God sees what you cannot. If you could know as God knows — fully, end from beginning, every detail into eternity — you would make the same decisions He has made. Know that for sure.

In your current adversity, do you believe that God has the power to have prevented it?

Do you believe that God has the power to correct it immediately?

How does that make you feel about your current situation? Be honest. God will not be offended.

Can you find your way to accepting your adversity as it is right now is God's work in your life, working out a good and beneficial outcome?

Have you had any glimpses of what God is working into you in this experience?

DAY 3

HONESTLY

Don't be afraid to be honest with God. Listen to what Job said when he felt disillusioned with God: "I will give free rein to my complaint and speak out in the bitterness of my soul" (Job 10:1). God did not condemn Job for his openness, but instead complimented him for speaking rightly (42:7–8). It was Job's honesty with himself before God that opened the way for God to reach him with the truth.

As you begin this journey to understand how to live a praying life in adversity, what past experiences with prayer are holding you back? Stop now and name them.

Commit all these experiences, struggles, and longings to the Father. Don't let them hold you back any longer. Instead, let them propel you forward. Invite God to use these experiences as entry points where He can bring light. Trust Him. He is the one and only Guide on your faith walk, and it is His joy and delight to lead you in the ways of faith. "Do not be afraid, little flock, for your Father has been pleased to give you the kingdom" (Luke 12:32).

THINGS WILL NOT STAY AS THEY ARE RIGHT NOW

If you have been able to come to terms with your current situation and know that God is both loving and all-powerful at the same time, then prayer and its effects will make more sense. Prayer makes a difference. The purpose of prayer is to change the earth. Prayer matters.

James 5:16–18 makes a bold statement about prayer. It tells us that prayer changes the earth. It tells us that the spiritual power that prayer releases has authority over the earth. The earth is subject to the power of the Spirit.

"The prayer of a righteous person is powerful and effective" (James 5:16). The word translated "powerful and effective" is a Greek word that means "to exercise force; to create change." Prayer has power, and prayer produces an effect.

Your prayers in your adverse situation are changing things. You may not see the change with your eyes, but you can know with your faith. Prayer always does what God promises it will do: it always releases the power and provision of God. God's power and provision creates change.

That change is likely happening in a realm you can't observe. Prayer has its first effect in the spiritual end of reality. Prayer has stirred up great activity in the heavenly realms. The spiritual realm is where all matters are settled and all warfare won. That which is accomplished in the spiritual realm is then revealed on the earth.

Spirit is the cause of the material realm (Hebrews 11:3) and is the genesis of activity on the earth. Earth is the reflection or the shadow of activity occurring in the spiritual realm.

For example, Paul teaches us in Ephesians 6:12 that our enemies are not flesh and blood. Rather, they are powers and principalities in the heavenly realms. It would appear that flesh and blood — people — are standing in the way of God's purposes. But Scripture tells us that what we see on the earth is the result of what is happening in the heavenly realms. We also learn that the remedy for what is happening on earth will be accomplished in the spiritual realm. Victories in the spiritual realm result in changes in the physical realm. Earth is subject to the powers of spirit.

Because of prayer, you can be certain that change is being brought about in the spiritual realm, whether or not you can see the change on earth yet. Also, change is occurring on earth in places you can't see because they are not in your scope. Changes are occurring inside people. You can't see inside people. We often look at the outside and think we see the inside. What happens deep inside a person will take some time to be worked to the outside. Another way change is occurring is circumstances that are not part of your experience. Things are happening in situations you don't even know about that will eventually impact the situation in your life.

For years Sue prayed for her wayward son. His life was going in all the wrong directions, and for all she could see, it was getting worse and worse. She watched and scrutinized his life for signs of change. She evaluated every word he spoke, hoping to see change. No change seemed apparent. Things seemed to be going downhill. It seemed that prayer was making no difference at all. Then, one day — out of the blue, it seemed — he called and wanted to see her. He had news to share. He told her of his gradual conversion over the past several years from an agnostic cynic to a newly born-again believer.

Change had been happening over years? While she looked for change and couldn't see it? As it turned out, he had started working out at a gym with a trainer who led a Bible study at the gym for his clients. Her son had attended out of curiosity, and had been pulled in by the attitudes of the men and the clear teaching, and over the past two years had been progressively embracing belief until he reached a point of complete surrender. She could see no sign of it, but it was happening.

INVISIBLE BECOMES VISIBLE

This is how God has always worked. What you need is already available. God is not scrambling to come up with a plan. Instead, He is working a plan that has been from the beginning. He is not creating new supply for you. Rather, everything you need already exists in the spiritual realm, the heavens. I'll go into more detail on this in the next chapter. The prayer of faith is moving that which is available in the spiritual realm — the invisible realm — into the material realm. Prayer is the conduit by which God's power and provision come from heaven to earth. Prayer is God's word expressed through your mouth. He creates the impetus to pray. He pours His heart into yours, creating the content of prayer. For any given purpose — including prayer — God can place His words in your mouth. "Then the LORD reached out his hand and touched my mouth and said to me, 'I have put my words in your mouth'" (Jeremiah 1:9). He does this by creating His desires in your heart. The heart speaks from the overflow of the heart.

Let's look at how this has been God's way of working. His Word moves the invisible into the visible. When God speaks, that which is invisible takes on earthly substance. That which is in the spiritual realm moves into the earthly realm.

When God created the elements of earth, each element pictured an eternal reality. Most of the words — in the Greek, Hebrew, and Aramaic — that describe the creating process are words that foundationally mean "to order, to arrange, to fit one piece with another." Nothing random or impulsive about creation. It is a detailed, careful arrangement and a description of spiritual reality. When God created light, for example, He was creating a symbol of an eternal principle. Light, as earth knows it, exists because in eternity there is Light. When God gave Moses the instructions for building the tabernacle, He told Moses to be sure to follow the instructions to the last detail because he was making a model of a reality that existed in the heavenly realms. I believe that is what every atom of earth is — a model of a reality that exists in the eternal realm.

What was the reason God worked this way? So that we would always understand, by faith, that what is invisible and in the spiritual realm will be made visible in the earthly realm by the Word of God. He "calls into being things that were not" (Romans 4:17). The word *calls* means "to call out loud; to summon." He calls out loud to things that are invisible and commands them to be visible. He summons things in the spiritual realm and they move into the material realm.

DAY 4

CREATED AND SUSTAINED

Paul describes Jesus as "sustaining all things by his powerful word" (Hebrews 1:3). What holds everything together? What glues atom to atom and cell to cell? The dynamic, explosive power (*dunamis*) of Jesus' word (*rhema*) — His now speaking voiced word. If Jesus were not speaking out every moment, then the earth and all creation would fly apart. "All things were created through him and for him. He is before all things, and in him *all things hold together*" (Colossians 1:16–18; author's emphasis).

The very structure of the universe repeats this fact over and over, calling it out to every corner of creation. In the material creation, what is the force that holds all matter together? (Matter is anything that takes up space and has weight.) What is the force that holds the solar system together and forces it into its perfect rotation? The answer is gravity. Gravity is the ultimate mystery. Let me quote from an article entitled "The Eleven Greatest Unanswered Questions of Physics," written by Eric Haseltine for *Discover* magazine (February 2002): "All the ordinary matter we can find accounts for only about 4 percent of the universe. We know this by calculating how much mass would be needed to hold galaxies together and cause them to move about the way they do when they gather in large clusters. Another way to weigh the unseen matter is to look at how gravity bends the light from distant objects. Every measure tells astronomers that most of the universe is invisible."

Here is the mystery. Gravity is created by mass. The heavier the mass, the stronger gravitational force it creates. When scientists add up all the mass in the universe — the weight of all the planets and suns and moons and stars and little floating specs like neutrinos — the universe does not weigh enough to account for all the gravity that exists and holds it together. So what holds the universe together? The voice of Jesus calling life and order into the universe.

In another article from *Discover,* called "The Glue That Holds the World Together," Robert Kunzig wrote this:

> *You do not know what stuff is, you who hold it in your hands. Atoms? Yes, stuff is made of atoms. And every atom is a nucleus orbited by electrons. Every nucleus is built of protons. Every proton is — but there you reach the end of the line. Inside the proton lies the deep, unsettling truth: Stuff is made of nothing, or almost nothing, held together by glue, lots of glue.*

The "glue" to which Kunzig refers in this article are subatomic particles called gluons and they hold neutrinos together, which hold atoms together. When you reduce it all down, all matter is made of invisible energy or power.

Some years ago, scientists believed that matter was solid and static. That was before the discovery of the true structure of the atom. Actually, matter is made of up billions and billions of microscopic systems called atoms. An atom is in constant motion. In each atom, electrons orbit around a nucleus. The nucleus is made up of protons and neutrons strongly bound together. When the atom is split, the incredible force that binds the protons and neutrons together is released, and we have atomic energy. So, when matter is reduced to its smallest element — particles orbiting inside an atom — and that atom is split, what remains? Pure energy — power. What is the power that holds the atom's nucleus together — the power that is released when it is split? What is the power that binds atom to atom? No one knows. But the Scripture says that Jesus holds the universe together with His powerful present-tense word.

All matter is being held together by the force of subatomic (smaller than an atom) particles that are in continual high-speed motion. The air around you is not empty. It, too, is made up of atoms in motion. When sounds are made — when you speak, for example — the sound of your voice causes a positional change in the air molecules. It sets off a sound wave. By means of a sound wave, the energy introduced into the air molecules creates a wave effect in the air molecules around them, and the effect moves outward progressively in a wave. So, see if you agree with me that God's creation tells this story: God spoke and, by His act of speaking, an incomprehensible power set all matter into place, infusing it with life and order. He continues to speak, and the eternal sound waves of His voice keep the tiniest particles of matter moving in their rhythms, holding His creation together.

Scientists who study physics and the structures that make up the universe continue to be astounded as each discovery leads them back to the reality that matter, at its core, is some invisible force. Robert Kunzig, in the *Discover* article quoted earlier, ends his article with a quote from respected scientist Frank Wilczek: "If you really study the equations, it gets almost mystical."

Scientists agree that the amount of matter on the earth never changes. Matter changes forms. Water, for example, may transform into gas. A mountain may be eroded by a river, but the mountain's mass has now taken up residence in the water. Everything that God originally spoke into being still is. His word stands firm and immovable. No one can subtract from it or add to it. His invisible word created every visible element. His invisible word still brings His invisible power into view in the visible realm.

This word — this powerful, creating, sustaining word — is the same word He speaks into your heart and puts in your mouth. His word doing His work. That's what makes prayer powerful. His word through your mouth as prayer is changing things. How could it not?

CHANGED

Prayer is changing things. More than anything, prayer is changing you.

Through every situation, good or bad, you are being transformed. You are learning to let go of your own best ideas and open your life to His best ideas. You are learning that God is your only refuge. You are being freed from attitudes that have held you hostage. You are being released from the belief that happiness comes only when all circumstances line up to suit you. God is changing you in ways you didn't even know you needed to be changed. You are learning the freedom of surrender. Your heart is being tenderized in places that will show up later. You are becoming tender where you used to be calloused. You are learning mercy where you used to be filled with judgment. You are learning to embrace where you used to reject. Pride is crumbling — pride you didn't even know was there. Pride gets in God's way, so its destruction is opening a new way for God's power and glory to rule. Embrace it.

—〰—

Propelled by Grief into God's Embrace
Rachel Holley tells this story about how heartache at first shook her, but then became the impetus for deep and lasting change.

"Ask and it will be given to you; seek and you will find; knock and the door will be opened to you. For everyone who asks receives; the one who seeks finds; and to the one who knocks, the door will be opened" (Matthew 7:7–8).

I have a recurring memory that has helped me understand the "Why me?"; the "What did I do to deserve this?"; the "This cannot be my life; this was not the plan." This memory is all about a doctor's office and a parking lot. It is February 6, 1998, the day I found out that my third son had silently passed away in utero — no reason, healthy pregnancy. "Just happens sometimes," the doctor said. "Not all babies make it." I was so completely unprepared, this possibility being completely outside my frame of reference, that I believe I was in some sort of shock when my husband and I walked out of the doctor's office after getting the news.

I remember walking from the office, past nurses and receptionists talking on phones, tapping on computers. I remember people in the waiting room flipping through magazines, chatting. And then, to the elevator, pushing buttons, down to first floor where people milled around, headed for their own appointments, bought lattes or mochas at the little coffee stand. And then we went out revolving doors into the parking lot where cars came and went, where people parked or left for their respective homes. And as I moved through the ongoing life, I simply couldn't make sense of what was happening, as in, "How can all these people do what they're doing? The parking, the coffee, the phoning, the flipping through magazines? Don't they know, don't they comprehend what has just happened here? What is the matter with them? How can they just go on?"

This memory has meaning for me because of the way it has changed for me in the past 15 years; it has become a reminder of the answers to "Why me?" and the "This cannot be!" because it symbolizes the way I learned to manage life tragedy, the way I learned to continue walking into the world, like walking into the parking lot, the way I learned to participate in the world, despite the occurrence of something shocking, horrific, outside my frame of reference.

Because what started with Joseph's death would snowball, would avalanche, into a series of life tragedies for me, for my family, resulting in the loss of my marriage, my health, my children's well-being, our financial security, my career, relationships with family and friends, my self-respect, my reputation, and my self-confidence.

And this life trajectory simply wasn't supposed to be, at least in my mind, because I'd done everything right — come from a good family, dutifully gotten baptized, always went to church. I married a man I met in seminary, we had two beautiful boys, the house, the cars, good jobs, good friends. We had the onward and upward direction, the high hopes, expectations. And after my husband completed his doctorate, we moved to Anchorage, Alaska, for his first position as a university professor.

And it was the decision to go and the surprising event of a baby's death not long after we moved that changed the road I was traveling — no more onward and upward, no more high hopes. I was moving another direction now, one I never could have envisioned for myself.

Soon after the funeral, after family members left, I began trying to cope — I began to cope through various means — first doctors, and then counselors, spiritual directors, self-help books, too much exercise, or too much sleep. Then I took pills and more pills, finally alcohol, as much as I needed to stay numb. I knew I had to trudge through my days, do the *mundane chores, parent my two little boys, pretend to perform at my job daily, while functionally high, drunk. . . . Eighteen months after Joseph's death, our marriage was finished, an event I had few feelings about, since my husband had been absent since the baby's death anyway, spending all his time at work. I suppose it was his way of grieving.*

I think of the message of Matthew 7:7: seek and you'll find; ask and you'll receive; knock and the door will be opened. And when my life began to break apart, I sought, I asked, I knocked. I was seeking the selfish things I needed to feel better — rescue, escape, new circumstances, a change in situation — anything so I would be happier. And I was asking God for all these things I wanted, things which would get me through my grief and pain as soon as possible, things which would keep my children from being damaged by my breaking apart, things which would make my husband be what I wanted him to be — again, all things for me. And I knocked on God's door in the same way, "Let me in, and give me what I want! You promised!" I had always prayed this way — it took the unexpected events I used to call tragedies or adversity to find what I sought, to receive answers that I needed, to enter a new room.

I've heard many theories about tragic things happening to good people (e.g., God is working to make us stronger, God is teaching us something, God is testing our faith). For me, what rings true is something else. Looking at the whole of it today, what amounted to about 15 years of trying unsuccessfully to heal from all that happened, I see that when I was content, feeling secure, feeling as if nothing could go wrong — not to me — when I was complacent and satisfied, serene in my knowledge that while bad things happen, they didn't happen to me, I was conducting a surface relationship with God. I was knocking on the door but not really going in. It took adversity, it took tragedy, it took falling apart and being broken to propel me to God in a genuine way, to seek, to ask, to knock, but to do so from a selfless position of humility rather than a selfish position of entitlement.

From the moment I learned of Joseph's death, I began the process of being propelled toward God. The sadder, the sicker, the more dysfunctional I became, the more desperate I was to be different, feel better, heal. I wanted God things, comfort instead of peace, joy, hope. But of course,

I wanted to get them my way, telling God what I needed Him to do to make it all right, year after year. When He didn't give me what I wanted fast enough, I took matters into my own hands. But even so, I was being moved, because of these circumstances, toward God. I didn't know this at the time — I thought God had abandoned me — but instead, He was moving me through, and the seeking, the asking, the doors I knocked upon — alcohol, drugs, avoidance, depression, lying, pretending, escaping, numbing, isolating — all these things were the wrong doors, the wrong questions, the wrong treasures sought. But when I eventually broke, I was finally able to see and hear God. As someone who finally admitted brokenness, I was able to ask, "What do I need to do to be healed? I'll do anything You say, no matter what." I was able to seek, "What is Your will for me right this minute and the next and the next? Because relying on my own will has been a really lousy idea." And I was able to knock and hear, "Come on in. I've been with you all along."

When Joseph died, I was no part of the life happening around me in my vivid memory, the doctor's office parking lot. That memory — my analogy for dying and coming back to life. Resurrection through brokenness, through tragedy, through adversity. If Joseph were here, he'd be almost 16, tall, smart, and funny, like his older brothers. And I would thank him for his presence in the world; I would thank him for guiding me back into God's fold, back into the world of people, relationships, and actions God asks of us, His will.

Can you see any ways that you are changing as you walk out this adversity?

Have you been resisting the change, thinking God should correct the circumstance so you would not have to embrace painful — or humiliating — change?

Can you right now make this your prayer: *I accept and embrace any way that You want to change me, Father. I want You to have free rein in my life, and I know You are only changing me so that all of You will have access to all of me.*

DAY 5

PRAYER IS GOD'S STRATEGY

God has called us to pray because prayer is His strategy. He set prayer up to be the conduit through which the power and provision of heaven invade the environment and circumstances of earth. He has called us to pray, and that call is not in vain. He is not calling us to empty hope. He calls on us to pray because prayer makes a difference. Situations will change course because of prayer.

Prayer can change the attitudes of the person for whom you are praying more effectively than your best and brightest and most persuasive words. Prayer can penetrate into the very depths of a heart that you and I can never reach. Prayer releases the power of God into situations that are impenetrable to all our best efforts.

Prayer in adversity is going to require a stubborn faith. It will require perseverance. Jesus' most oft-repeated theme when He taught on prayer was perseverance.

The Word of God teaches that prayer—true prayer—is a long-term commitment. Jesus' teaching about prayer was, "Keep on asking and it will be given you; keep on seeking and you will find; keep on knocking . . . and [the door] will be opened to you" (Matthew 7:7 AMP). He teaches tenacity and perseverance. He told parables that illustrated persistent, persevering prayer. In one of His parables, He described a widow who came to an unjust judge over and over again until she received what she needed (Luke 18:1–8). Luke introduces this parable with these words: "Then Jesus told his disciples a parable to show them that they should always pray and not give up" (v. 1). The whole point of Jesus' parable was to teach us not to give up. Why did Jesus think it necessary to teach such a thing? Because He knew that prayer would require significant steadfastness and resolve. These requirements, if misunderstood, could make a person give up. He taught us that when we feel like giving up, we must resist doing so. Prayer is not for quitters.

When you feel like giving up, don't give up. When all you see indicates that prayer is not working, look past all you can see. Paul admonishes us to "fix our eyes not on what is seen, but on what is unseen, since what is seen is temporary, but what is unseen is eternal" (2 Corinthians 4:18).

Prayer is accomplishing what God intends to accomplish, and He intends good. Does that mean you can be sure that prayer will produce exactly the outcome you have scripted? God's plan will not necessarily look like you thought it should. You won't be able to "believe God into" doing your will.

Let's look at the experience of the person who says something like, "I had faith that God would do a certain thing, and then He didn't." You cannot have faith in an *outcome*. You can only have faith in a *person*. Jesus said, "Have faith *in God*" (Mark 11:22; author's emphasis).

Many times we pray in hopes that we will be able to manipulate circumstances and bring about our preferred outcome by means of faith expressed through prayer. Is that true of you, or am I the only one? That's where I began. I thought, *If I can learn how prayer operates, then I can get God to do what I think He should do when I think He should do it. If I can understand how prayer works, I can get everything to go my way.* Listen to the voice of experience: It doesn't work. That is a path fraught with disappointment. That kind of thinking is not faith. It is a flesh-fueled, fruitless endeavor. In that approach, we are still trying to control the circumstances according to our best ideas.

You can make yourself believe anything. What you believe does not have to be true. In the terrorist attacks against the United States on September 11, 2001, on Flight 92 that crashed outside Pittsburgh, Pennsylvania, the flight voice recorder recorded the terrorists screaming, "Allah Akbar!" as they plummeted to their death. In a shootout in Pakistan between alleged terrorists and the police, the news media reported the dying terrorists wrote on the walls in their blood as they died, "Allah Akbar!" They believed so fervently that they gave their lives. No one could have a stronger belief than the men I have just described. They believed something—a set of ideas, a theology.

Faith is not *believing something*. Faith is *believing Someone*. "Abraham believed God" (James 2:23). Faith is not marching in lock step with a set of beliefs. It is not giving intellectual assent to a doctrinal position. Faith is focused on God. Prayer is not about belief in an outcome; rather, prayer is about faith in God.

Have you scripted an outcome for your situation? Can you lay it down right now and trust God completely? Write out how you are feeling right now.

PRAYER'S POWER

As I write, I'm trying to balance two realities. The first, prayer is powerful. How much power does prayer have? It has all the power of heaven.

God's power—the power released by prayer—is power that has a direct and observable impact on the earth. Paul describes the power available through prayer in Ephesians 1:19–20 (NIV 1984): "His incomparably great power for us who believe. That power is like the working of his mighty strength, which he exerted in Christ when he raised him from the dead and seated him at his right hand in the heavenly realms."

Paul is describing heaven's power released by prayer—the power that flows in response to every prayer you pray, and every prayer you sigh. Let's look at his description closely. First it is "incomparably great." There is no comparison. Consider anything that you think of as having great power: tsunami, hurricane, raging fire. Anything. God's power is so great that we can't even draw a comparison. It is beyond measure.

Then the phrase, "the working of his mighty strength." Piling word upon word to convey the fullness of the power. "Working" is a translation of the Greek word from which we also get "energy." Power in action. The word translated "mighty" means an inherent or indwelling power. According to the *Theological Dictionary of the New Testament*, its definition is: "Denoting the presence and significance of force or strength rather than its exercise." The word for "strength" means the capability, or the ability. So, string it together and it might be like this.

Let's imagine that I'm standing in front of you, just being me. And let's imagine that "me" is very strong. There I stand, strong. That's my might. Then let's imagine that I flex my muscles, so you can see my capability. When you look at my big muscles, you can observe that I would be able to accomplish much. That's my strength. Now, when I pick up a table and throw it across the room — that would be the working of my mighty strength.

Prayer accesses the working of God's mighty strength. The power of prayer has no limits, no boundaries. Prayer gives unrestricted access to heaven's power. Prayer is powerful and effective. It produces change.

The second reality I'm balancing here is that prayer is not a vending machine. You don't put in a prayer and get out an answer. Though it will always, without fail, access the power of heaven, that power in operation will often not look like you or I might have prescribed that it should look.

Prayer will work as God intends for it to work when it becomes what God intends for it to be. Prayer is not an activity, but a relationship. Prayer is not a formula, but a life. Only when we have learned how to live prayer, breathe prayer, be prayer — only then will the power available through prayer be consistently manifested on the earth. God has ordained that prayer will be the conduit through which His intervening, earth-changing power flows from heaven to earth. Prayer is what sets God's will in motion on the earth.

WEEK 2

THE PROCESS OF PRAYER

As you are learning to live a praying life, prayer takes on a much broader definition than "saying prayers." Much of what prayer is accomplishing cannot be condensed to a list. Many times the direct answers to petitions are the least important aspect of what the prayer accomplished. I believe that as you progress and mature into a praying life, your testimony of prayer's effectiveness will be that the mercies of God unfold at every turn. You walk in answered prayer. O. Hallesby states it like this: "The longer you live a life of this kind, the more answers to prayer you will experience. As white snow flakes fall quietly and thickly on a winter's day, answers to prayer will settle down on you at every step you take, even to your dying day."

It is during the process of prayer that God does His mightiest work. If this were not so, then God would have set prayer up to work like a vending machine: put in a request, get out an answer. God has a loving and productive reason for the process of prayer.

—Live a Praying Life®: Open Your Life to God's Power and Provision

DAY I

Life is punctuated with pain. Believer or nonbeliever, earth is not heaven. You can't escape challenges and difficulties. But, as believers, through prayer, we can let every adversity be God's tool for enriching us and deepening us and healing us. What should be to our detriment becomes our greatest good.

As you live a praying life in adversity, you will discover that the prayer process God has designed leads you to more freedom, deeper joy, and greater peace. He has designed prayer to work in the context of relationship. He is not a filling station. Quick stops for a fill-up until the next time you feel the need for Him will not bring into your life all that He has for you. His invitation is not to stop in any time, but rather to abide. Move in. Put down roots. Stay. Remain. Out of the life that is abandoned to God and His purposes flows the prayer that God has promised to answer.

"Remain in me, as I also remain in you" (John 15:4).

THE FRUIT OF ABIDING

Jesus uses the beautiful metaphor of a vine and its branches to define what He means by "abiding."

"No branch can bear fruit by itself; it must remain in the vine. Neither can you bear fruit unless you remain in me. I am the vine; you are the branches. If you remain in me and I in you, you will bear much fruit; apart from me you can do nothing" (vv. 4–5).

The branches have been grafted into the vine, and if the graft takes — if the branch remains — then the vine's life flows into the branch and becomes its new life. That branch used to be part of another branch that produced other fruit, but it has been cut off from that vine. It has died to the old life. Now it has become one with the new vine and the life of the new vine produces its fruit through that branch. The branch that died to the old vine has been resurrected in the new vine.

You see the picture, don't you? Jesus has taken us into Himself, filled us with His life. That life flows continually, not sporadically. The branch just abides while the vine's life flows.

He makes this promise to the branch that abides. "Ask whatever you wish, and it will be done for you" (v. 7). The prerequisite to the promise? "If you remain in me and my words remain in you, ask . . ."

And the fruit He promises? "This is to my Father's glory, that you bear much fruit, showing yourselves to be my disciples" (v. 8; author's emphasis).

"If you remain in me and my words remain in you, ask whatever you wish, and it will be done for you. This is to my Father's glory, that you bear much fruit, showing yourselves to be my disciples" (John 15:7–8).

Using these words from Scripture as your guide, respond to the following.

1. Write out the if/then statement (the "then" is implied):
   If _____
   Then _____

2. In an if/then statement, the "if" clause causes the "then" clause. Explain the relationship between the "if" and the "then" in this statement.

3. *If* you soak yourself in His Word and let it live in you, *then* you will experience answers to prayer. Is that what you saw? His Word actively works in you to create His desires. "It is God who works in you to will . . . his good purpose" (Philippians 2:13).

The next sentence in John 15:8 builds on that understanding: "This is to my Father's glory." What is to His Father's glory? Go back to the sentence upon which He is building.

4. What is to His Father's glory? Answered prayer! Why? What does answered prayer do? Look at the next phrase: "that you bear much fruit, showing yourself to be my disciples." Fruit always means an outer result of an inner work. What is the fruit He has been talking about here?

5. The fruit here is answered prayer. How will answered prayer prove that you are Jesus' disciple?

His life flowing through me creates desires that match His. If He is flowing in me like the vine's life in the branch, then He is molding and shaping my prayers.

"This is to my Father's glory." What is to His Father's glory? Answered prayer!

Answered prayer is the fruit of the Vine's life through the branch. It is the authenticating mark of the present-tense life of Christ in me. The fruit on a branch identifies what kind of vine it is. You know a tree by its fruit. The life of Christ flowing through you creates the desires of Christ in you, which produces the will of Christ through you in the form of answered prayer.

During the process of prayer, He is moving in you, through you, recreating the landscape of your soul. He is reproducing His heart in you, and His prayers through you. During the process of prayer, He is bringing your will into natural alignment with His.

You just read in John 15:7, "Ask whatever you wish, and it will be done for you." Ask whatever you will (desire). Now read this statement in 1 John 5:14–15:

This is the confidence we have in approaching God: that if we ask anything according to his will, he hears us. And if we know that he hears us — whatever we ask — we know that we have what we asked of him.

Ask whatever He wills (desires).

On the surface, these two statements seem to contradict one another. However, the reality of a praying life brings these two contradictory statements together as one truth. Both statements are true at the same time. In a praying life, the living, indwelling, present-tense Jesus is in you, His word dwelling in you in richly (see Colossians 3:16). He embodies His word — His message. His word lives in you and makes itself at home in you. *The Message* states it this way: "Let the Word of Christ — the Message — have the run of the house. Give it plenty of room in your lives."

In the praying life, the seeming contradictions are resolved. Here's how Oswald Chambers puts it in his book *Christian Disciplines*: "The Holy Spirit not only brings us into the zone of God's influence but into intimate relationship with Him personally, so that by the slow discipline of prayer the choices of our free will become the preordinations of His almighty order."

Powerful praying occurs when:

1. I allow Him to align my thoughts and purposes with His.

2. I give up my preconceived ideas of what I want and need and allow Him to fill me with His abundance.

3. I bring my will into active cooperation with His.

4. My mind, will, and emotions become the conduits through which

He can express His thoughts, desires, and longings.

As He lives in you, embodying the Word, He is transforming your heart to reflect His. He is making direct deposits from His mind into yours. What you will and what He wills are becoming one and the same. This is always in process, not finished. But more and more each day, each moment, it becomes more completed.

THE SECRETS TO ABIDING

"If . . . my words remain in you." The first secret to abiding is to marinate your life in His Word. In living a praying life, we learn how to hear Him as He speaks His word in present tense to us. His word is living and active. It does His work.

Faith has a foundation, a resting place. The Word of God is faith's birthplace. God Himself is the focus of faith, and His Word is the way that He reveals Himself to us. His Word is the method by which He discloses His innermost thoughts. By His Word, His mind—His reasoning, His purposes, His desires—become accessible to us.

God's Word lays an excellent foundation for your faith. In His Word, He proclaims what He intends to do and describes what He has available to give. Unless we interact with His living Word continually, our faith will have nowhere to put down roots.

His Word is living, active, powerful, creative. It is not stagnant and static. God is a speaking God who is always speaking in present tense. The Scripture opens and the One True God is introduced to mankind as a speaking God, speaking words that create life and order.

In the beginning God created the heavens and the earth. Now the earth was formless and empty, darkness was over the surface of the deep, and the Spirit of God was hovering over the waters. And God said, "Let there be light," and there was light (Genesis 1:1–3).

Hebrew Torah scholars teach that whatever God reveals first is what is primary and foundational. Everything subsequently revealed must be understood as building upon the first thing to be revealed. The very first mention of God tells us that He is a creating God who does His work by His now speaking word. Light came into being at His word — at the moment of His speaking, as immediate response to His voice. Every living thing exists because of the word that proceeded from the mouth of God.

As Jesus faced down His enemy in the desert, remember that Jesus referred to "every word that proceeds out of the mouth of God" (Matthew 4:4 NASB). Jesus is quoting the Scripture, and He no doubt said it either in the Hebrew in which it was written, or in the Aramaic language (closely akin to Hebrew) that Jesus and His contemporaries spoke. The wording in the oldest Greek renderings available to us say something like, "Every single *rhema* [present, voiced word] that flows like a river through the mouth of God." The Greek word *ekporeuomai* — "flows out of or comes forth from" — is in the present tense and active voice. It is happening in real time. Right now. At this moment. Man lives by the words that God is speaking right now.

Let's look at the Scripture Jesus was quoting. "Man does not live on bread alone but on every word that comes from the mouth of the LORD" (Deuteronomy 8:3). In Hebrew culture, most Jewish people knew much of the Scripture by heart. People commonly communicated by quoting a portion of a Scripture or the opening words and the closing words of a passage, implying the whole passage. It is like when one person steeped in American culture and language says to another, "If the shoe fits . . ." or "When in Rome . . ." Confident of his hearer's familiarity with the phrase, the speaker is communicating the entire phrase by stating a portion of it. When Jesus spoke the words of Deuteronomy 8:3 to His enemy, He was implying the whole thought. Let's look at it.

"He humbled you, causing you to hunger and then feeding you with manna, which neither you nor your fathers had known, to teach you that man does not live on bread alone but on every word that comes from the mouth of the LORD" (v. 3).

God put the Israelites in a position where they would experience hunger *so that* He could feed them with manna *for the purpose of* teaching them that they could live on what flows from the mouth of God. What was manna? It was the bread that came out of heaven and caused them to live. In the Hebrew, *word* is not in the text. It has been inserted by translators. The Hebrew says, "By every single thing, every sort of thing, that flows like a river through the mouth of God." What proceeded from the mouth of God? Manna! That's right, manna came from the mouth of God. Somewhere in the heavens, God said, "Let there be manna," and there was manna. Manna was the spoken word of God in an earthly form. Manna existed because God spoke it. The Israelites lived by the manna that God spoke into being—the word that proceeded out of His mouth.

Jesus had just spent 40 days and 40 nights fasting in the desert. He was saying to His enemy, "God has allowed Me to experience the reality that My spirit and My innermost being is nourished and given life by what God is feeding Me—His living word voiced to Me in the present tense. Everything that My body needs, God will speak into My life."

In this time of adversity in your life, how has God been supplying what you need for each day? Don't describe your situation in terms of what you don't have, but rather describe it in terms of what you do have.

You are still standing. You haven't been defeated by the weight of your sorrow. What gives you strength to take on another day? Do you see God's activity speaking His present word, "Let there be," into your life and heart?

Your faith is resting on the foundation of the word of God. But don't make the mistake of confining your idea of the word of God to something He said in the past and that continues to have relevance today. The word of God is something He is always speaking in the present tense. His word is living and active and now.

The Scripture is the living Word of God, so even those passages addressed to a particular audience in a specific time regarding a unique event have layers of meaning. Even those passages that are spoken within the context of time echo into eternity, speaking fresh truth to God's people in any given moment.

THE NATURE OF GOD'S WORD

As we start to look closely at God's Word, keep in mind the nature of His word. First, remember that it is flowing right out of the depths of God. Second, remember that anything that God speaks is brought into being by the very act of His speaking. If God says, "Let there be light," there is light. If He says, "Let there be manna," there is manna. And third, remember that His Word is eternal and it is "the last word." Nothing can override it or undermine it. His word is the "amen" to all His promises — the "it is so; so let it be."

Through His Word, God intends to reveal His will to us. He means for us to know what is available and what He desires to put into our lives. It is not His plan to keep us in the dark, but instead He wants to bring us into His inner circle where He can tell us His secrets. Listen to Jesus say this to you right now: "I no longer call you servants, because a servant does not know his master's business. Instead, I have called you friends, for *everything* that I learned from my Father I have made known to you" (John 15:15-16; author's emphasis).

Let's look at the eternal record and see what is proceeding from the mouth of God about knowing His desires.

First, remember 1 John 5:14-15, and look for the key to experiencing consistently the power and provision of God in response to your prayers.

This is the confidence we have in approaching God: that if we ask anything according to his will, he hears us. And if we know that he hears us — whatever we ask — we know that we have what we have asked of him."

Do you see? We can have absolute and unwavering confidence that we have what we have asked for *when we know we are asking according to His will.*

Is there a catch? Is this just a bait and switch? If God says that the key to answered prayer is to ask according to His will, then He must have made it possible to know His will.

God's will is a mystery, but it is a mystery that He has revealed. In Colossians 1:25–26, Paul says that God had given him a commission "to present to you the word of God in its fullness — the mystery that has been kept hidden for ages and generations, but is now disclosed to the Lord's people." Paul is saying that the abundant riches God has available had been disguised or hidden or kept secret for ages and generations. God had intentionally not allowed the fullness of His provision to be known. But all that has changed. Now the Word of God (Paul means the Old Testament) can be announced in its fullness — all the layers exposed and all the pictures brought to life. "To them God has chosen to make known among the Gentiles the glorious riches of this mystery, which is Christ in you, the hope of glory" (v. 27). The mystery and all its fullness and all its abundance is summed up in these three words: "Christ in you." You could summarize this passage of Paul's letter like this: God's will that was once hidden is now revealed.

Time and time again, Scripture refers to the mystery of His will, once hidden but now revealed. In Romans, Paul talks about "the revelation of the mystery hidden for long ages past, but now revealed and made known through the prophetic writings by the command of the eternal God, so that all the Gentiles might come to the obedience that comes from faith" (16:25–26). The prophetic writings were in place, but the deep mystery of God's will contained in them has only been revealed since the Spirit came to indwell believers. The mystery of His will is now revealed.

Look at Paul's prayer recorded in the Book of Colossians, "So that they may have the *full riches of complete understanding,* in order that they may know the mystery of God, namely, Christ, *in whom are hidden all the treasures of wisdom and knowledge*" (2:2–3; author's emphasis). Once you have Christ and have come to understand God's plan — His revealed mystery of Christ in you — then you have access to all the wisdom and knowledge of God because God's will is embodied in Jesus. You've got Jesus? Then you have the storehouse of all the desires of God. Your salvation includes everything about your new, eternal quality of life. Your salvation is not just what happens to you after your body dies.

The path His will takes, the way He brings His will into being, remains a mystery. "Oh, the depth of the riches of the wisdom and knowledge of God! How unsearchable his judgments, and his paths beyond tracing out!" (Romans 11:33). God will never hand over to us His all-knowingness. Sometimes we mistake His will for His ways and become confused. When I think that I have reached an understanding of God's will and begin to pray according to it, He often begins bringing His will about in a way that looks, to me, like a mistake. I have now built up enough history with Him that usually I know to wait and watch — not to confuse His ways with His will. I'm learning not to confuse what He's doing with how He's doing it.

What looked more like the end of His desire to bring salvation through Jesus, the Messiah, than Jesus hanging on the Cross? What looked more like the end of His promise to Joseph than Joseph bound in chains in a prison in Egypt? What looked more like the end of Paul's mission than Paul beaten and imprisoned? What looked more like the end of Abraham's vision than his one and only son bound to an altar with a blade in its downward arc?

THE DEEP THINGS OF GOD

In 1 Corinthians 2:6–16, Paul writes a passage explaining how you and I can know the deep things of God. Before we start digesting these words, let me point you to Paul's Jewish understanding of the deep things of God. "He reveals deep and hidden things; he knows what lies in darkness, and light dwells with him" (Daniel 2:22). God knows truth that is deep (unsearchable) and hidden (kept secret). He alone knows these deep truths. At moments of His own choosing, He reveals those deep and hidden things to individuals. Paul, writing out of his Jewish mind-set, says:

We do, however, speak a message of wisdom among the mature, but not the wisdom of this age or of the rulers of this age, who are coming to nothing. No, we declare God's wisdom, a wisdom that has been hidden and that God destined for our glory before time began. None of the rulers of this age understood it, for if they had, they would not have crucified the Lord of glory. However, as it is written: "What no eye has seen, what no ear has heard, and what no human mind has conceived" — the things God has prepared for those who love him — these are the things God has revealed it to us by his Spirit.

The Spirit searches all things, even the deep things of God. For who knows a person's thoughts except their own spirit within them? In the same way no one knows the thoughts of God except the Spirit of God. What we have received is not the spirit of the world, but the Spirit who is from God, so that we may understand what God has freely given us. This is what we speak, not in words taught us by human wisdom but in words taught by the Spirit, explaining spiritual realities with Spirit-taught words. The person without the Spirit does not accept the things that come from the Spirit of God but considers them foolishness, and cannot understand them, because they are discerned only through the Spirit. The person with the Spirit makes judgments about all things, but such a person is not subject to any human judgments, for, "Who has known the mind of the Lord so as to instruct him? But we have the mind of Christ" (1 Corinthians 2:6–16; author's emphasis).

Paul says (my paraphrase), "I am speaking words to you that explain the wisdom that God has imparted to me about the deep and hidden things. This wisdom is completely divorced from what passes as wisdom among the rulers of this age — transient, time-framed thought rather than eternal truth. These God-authored words I'm speaking are bringing to light that which has been obscured since time began. This secret wisdom has always been destined for us, meant to bring us into glory by the indwelling life of Christ." Then he continues, explaining New Covenant reality. "The very things that have been hidden — the very things that no eye has seen, no ear has heard, and no mind has conceived — have now been revealed to us by the Spirit, who knows the depths of God. He instructs us in all the secret wisdom of the heavenly realms for this purpose: so that we will *understand what is available to us* — what God wills us to have."

God wants to reveal to you His deepest thoughts, tell you His best secrets. He wants to instruct you in His will. He wants to fill you up with the knowledge of His will.

To clarify, you won't know the details, or the exact way God's plan will look when it is revealed. You won't be God or have His full knowledge. But the Holy Spirit will impart to you all you need to know when you need to know it.

How does God's Word provide the firm foundation for your faith?

Are you convinced that God wants you to know His desires?

What is the difference between knowing what He wants to do and knowing how He wants to do it?

If you relinquish the need to know *how* He will bring His will into being, and rest in the reality that *He is* bringing His will about, what will change in your daily walk?

DAY 2

THE LIVING WORD LIVING IN YOU

"The Word became flesh and made his dwelling among us" (John 1:14).

Jesus is the Word of God. "In the beginning was the Word, and the Word was with God, and the Word was God. He was with God in the beginning" (vv. 1–2). He not only existed at the beginning but He also caused the beginning. "Through him all things were made; without him nothing was made that has been made" (v. 3).

The person of Jesus the Messiah embodies fully the Word of God. He *is* the Word. He is the Living Word that the written Word conveys, not the other way around. If there were no Living Word, then there would be no written Word to express Him. Without the eternal Living Word, there would be no word to be spoken. Because He *is*, therefore everything that exists *is*. "Without him nothing was made that has been made." The writer of Hebrews refers to the Son in this way: "through whom also he made the universe" (Hebrews 1:2). Paul describes Him this way:

For in him all things were created: things in heaven and on earth, visible and invisible, whether thrones or powers or rulers or authorities; all things have been created through him and for him. He is before all things, and in him all things hold together (Colossians 1:16–17).

The Apostle John opens his gospel with the very words that open the Scripture, "In the beginning." John says this: "When the beginning of creating occurred, the Word already was" (author's paraphrase). By opening his message with this most Hebraic phrasing and concept, I am convinced that John's whole message is to be interpreted in light of Hebrew concepts. Look at the Hebrew concept that was clearly in John's mind. John was boldly and clearly tying his introduction directly to the opening scenes of creation and the first words of Torah. This was not subtle. John meant for that connection to be made with no ambiguity. God created every cell and molecule by His Word. His Word is embodied in Jesus.

The Word has always been. The Word is. The Word will always be. And the Word lives in you. "The word is near you; it is in your mouth and in your heart" (Romans 10:8).

Everything that comes out of the heart and mind of God is housed in Jesus and Jesus is housed in you. What is the mystery that was kept hidden in the prophetic writings and revealed only in the New Covenant? What has God always been saying? What was the content of the Scripture from the beginning? Let me remind you.

"I have become its servant by the commission God gave me to present to you the word of God in its fullness — the mystery that has been kept hidden for ages and generations, but is now disclosed to the Lord's people. To them God has chosen to make known among the Gentiles the glorious riches of this mystery, which is Christ in you, *the hope of glory"* (Colossians 1:25–27; author's emphasis).

Mystery revealed in you. The Word dwelling in you. The Word speaking in you. The Word by which the universe was created makes His home in you. True to His nature, He is speaking truth and wisdom to you from inside you.

When you read the written Word, the Living Word speaks it to you. He speaks to you in present and specific ways, heart to heart. He presents His thoughts to your mind in a fashion that is tailored to your personality and experiences.

For all of us, He is right there in our present moment speaking life-altering truth in a direct transfer from His mind to ours. Why can He do that? Because "we have the mind of Christ" (1 Corinthians 2:16). Putting the meaning of the Greek words into the sentence, it says something like this: We have, as our own possession, the thoughts, intellect, judgment, and perceptions of Messiah. We have Messiah's thoughts in a present state — as He thinks them right now — as they are relevant to our moments and to our lives.

GOD'S REVELATION THROUGH JESUS

God has fully revealed Himself through Jesus. The word *logos* (translated "word") also means a declaration or a message. I've always thought it was interesting that God called Jesus the Message instead of the Messenger. A messenger is separate from the message. Once a messenger has delivered the message, he is no longer relevant. However, Jesus *is* the Message. He always has been the Message and always will be the Message. Apart from the Living Jesus, the mind, heart, and thoughts of God have no expression. They are inaccessible.

In John 16:12–15, Jesus says that everything the Father knows, Jesus knows. And the Spirit will take what Jesus knows and declare it to you.

Go back now and read the passage, considering each phrase and how one thought flows into the next. Do you see the whole thing?

I have much more to say to you, more than you can now bear. But when he, the Spirit of truth, comes, he will guide you into all the truth. He will not speak on his own; he will speak only what he hears, and he will tell you what is yet to come. He will glorify me because it is from me that he will receive what he will make known to you. All that belongs to the Father is mine. That is why I said the Spirit will receive from me what he will make known to you (John 16:12–15).

When will Jesus speak the "much more" He has to say?

How will the indwelling Jesus make known all that the Father has for you?

Jesus is the Word of God. He is always speaking to you from within by His Spirit. He speaks the Scripture into a present reality. He speaks personal and specific words of promise to you. He creates in you the desires of God for you. "For it is God who works *in you* to will and to act in order to fulfill his good purpose" (Philippians 2:13; author's emphasis).

Are you seeing that you can't separate the Living Word from the written Word? It is the Living Word who infuses the Scripture with Spirit and life.

MARINATE

Recognizing the importance of Scripture to lay a foundation for your faith, make every opportunity absorb it. Marinate your mind in it. When you marinate a cut of meat, you submerge the meat in the marinade. The marinade seeps into the meat, infusing the cells of the meat with its own flavor. It tenderizes the meat, breaking down tough sinew, making it palatable. The longer you let it marinate, the more effectively the marinade does its work. Marinate your mind in the Word of God. Keep your thoughts there, letting it do its transforming work.

Read, study, memorize, meditate. Sing the Word. Think on it as you fall asleep at night, and let it greet you first thing when you wake up. Read books that point you to the Word. Listen to teaching that gives sound instruction in the Word. Talk about it with fellow believers. Hang Scripture art on your walls.

I think technology has opened new ways to explore Scripture and feed on it continually. Let me tell you about two things I do. There are many Bible computer programs available. When I want to focus on a book or a section of Scripture, I copy and paste that section into a word-processing program. Then I double-space it and leave a wide margin on the right-hand side of the page. Often, I will copy the section from several different translations. Then I print it, three-hole-punch it, and put it in a notebook. Now I can write all over it, circle things, make notes in the margins, put sticky notes on it, draw pictures, or whatever I want to.

Another thing I do is read into a digital recorder the book or section of Scripture I am focusing on. I can read it with the emphasis and inflection I want it to have. Then I just listen to it as I'm falling asleep and let it play while I sleep. I'm convinced that your dreaming mind is influenced by things you are hearing while you sleep. I have a very scientific basis for this. One night I fell asleep with the television on. I dreamed a detailed dream, but woven throughout it was a recurring theme. No matter what else the actors in my dream were doing, they were all getting hair implants. I woke up to find that there was an infomercial for hair implants on the television. I thought, *Well, if information about hair implants can insert itself into my dreaming mind, then certainly the Word of God can.*

Scripture says the same thing. "I will bless the LORD who has counseled me; Indeed, my mind instructs me in the night" (Psalm 16:7 NASB). The Lord counsels me — teaches, advises, guides me — by His Word. Then my mind continues to receive that instruction even during the night. God has created your brain so that this is possible. When you go to sleep, the cognitive portion of your mind goes into a neutral state, and the subconscious part of your brain is predominant. Your subconscious mind does not have to follow all the many rules that your conscious mind does, so it can think in fresh and creative ways. All night long, your mind is sorting out new information and comparing it to old information. Brain scans show that when you are in your deepest sleep state, your brain is every bit as active as when you are wide awake. Researchers say that when you are learning new information, you have to sleep on it before your brain can fully assimilate it.

Often people tell me that they feel guilty because they fall asleep at night while they are praying. I say, "Have you ever heard of prayer sleeping?" You've heard of prayerwalking, right? Well, now you've heard of prayer sleeping. Go to sleep praying, you will be praying all through the night. You may wake up during the night with a person on your mind, or a song in your mind, or any number of indications that you have been prayer sleeping. When you wake up in the morning, you will be in a state of prayer. When you go to sleep listening to the Word, you are prayer sleeping. The Word of God is actively working in you and speaking to you all through the night, creating Spirit-formed prayer.

Soak your life in the Word. It is building a firm foundation for your faith. As God authors our prayers, He doesn't just dictate to us. He changes us. He redirects our thoughts. He reforms our attitudes. He reframes our memories so that we can see them from His perspective. As we purposefully keep our lives soaked in His presence, He will give Himself to us.

—⁓—

A Marinated Life

Marsha Boswell Brown tells how the unexpected blow that could have shattered her life, instead proved the faithfulness of God, who prepared her heart in advance for what He knew was coming, but she did not. How marinating her life in His Word meant she had the Living Word speaking His living words to her.

After 37 years of marriage, my husband told me one Sunday morning that he was leaving. He felt that we didn't really have a good marriage and that he would be happier away from me. I'll not bore you with all of the dismal details leading up to that morning, nor will I hang all his laundry out to dry. Suffice it to say, that is a devastating thing to hear from the man you love. From that moment, though, I was filled with the most amazing peace that is beyond understanding — truly inexplicable.

You see, all the ingredients that make up who I am, over time, under the heat of living the principles and truths of God's Word and the discipline of obedience to Him had simmered all those years to coalesce into how God's amazing grace got me through the days, weeks, and months following my husband leaving.

Key verses that had been mainstays throughout my life, came bubbling to the top of my consciousness not sometimes but every time *I needed them.*

"The Lord himself goes before you and will be with you; he will never leave you nor forsake you" *(Deuteronomy 31: 8).*

"Lean not unto your own understanding; in all your ways submit to him, and he will make your paths straight" *(Proverbs 3:5-6)*.

"My grace is sufficient for you, for my power is made perfect in weakness" *(2 Corinthians 12:9)*.

"Consider it pure joy . . . when you face trials of many kinds, because you know that the testing of your faith produces perseverance" *(James 1: 2-3)*.

"Rejoice always, pray continually, give thanks in all circumstances; for this is God's will for you in Christ Jesus" (1 Thessalonians 5:16–18).

"Rejoice in the Lord always. I will say it again: Rejoice! Let your gentleness be evident to all. The Lord is near. Do not be anxious about anything, but in situation, by prayer and petition, with thanksgiving, present your requests to God. And the peace of God, which transcends all understanding, will guard your hearts and your minds in Christ Jesus" *(Philippians 4:4-7)*.

All those verses and many more had been learned, memorized, thought about, talked about, and even written on tiles and calendars in my home. Through the years the principles of those verses were chopped, diced, sautéed, and simmered in the big stew pot I called my life. They guided me through raising two sons and all the ups and downs of parenting. They sustained me through sickness, depression, and gaining weight. They began to break down and enter my psyche during long illnesses of aging parents and in-laws. They were what I leaned on when two sons went to war.

That Sunday morning, when my heart was breaking, His grace was sufficient. I wasn't joyful, but through the boiling of a lifetime, I had learned the value of obedience, and as a sheer act of my will, I counted it joy and submitted to its working. I obeyed and gave thanks. I rejoiced.

Am I crazy-insane? Perhaps, but I have done this over and over — obeyed His Word. I had, throughout a lifetime, learned to be thankful and rejoice even when I did not feel like it. He has proved Himself faithful. Rejoicing and giving thanks leads to a peace that transcends understanding. It worked with little things like lost parking spaces and sore throats and disappointments over baseball games. Once again I obeyed. Through my tears, through that lump of ice in my chest, I told a loving heavenly Father that this was not what I wanted, and I could not understand why, but I would trust Him and let Him lead. I told Him I was not happy or thankful, but I would thank Him in this circumstance because He tells me in His Word to do so.

And, you know what? It works — the peace of God which transcends understanding filled my heart and has not left me one second. Oh, there have been difficult days. Meeting with a divorce attorney is a really sobering experience. Our anniversary, our birthdays, Christmas . . . were difficult times filled with stormy emotions. But in every weakness, every struggle, every sad day, His gentle whisper, "My grace is sufficient. I will never leave you, nor forsake you."

—⟨⟨⟩⟩—

DAY 3

OBEDIENCE

The second secret to abiding is living in obedience. Jesus continues His vine-and-branch teaching with this statement:

"As the Father has loved me, so have I loved you. Now remain in my love. If you keep my commands, you will remain in my love, just as I have kept my Father's commands and remain in his love. I have told you this so that my joy may be in you and that your joy may be complete" (John 15:9–11).

See that He is using that same word for "remain" or "abide." He is giving another secret for how He has lived His life abiding in the Father. He's not saying that if you don't obey He doesn't love you, but that when you don't obey, you don't live in the full experience of His love. His love does not change, but your experience of His love changes.

When you change from thinking of prayer as saying prayers, and instead begin to live a praying life, you realize that prayer is often expressed in obedience to what God is speaking now in your life through His Word. Obedience is the ultimate expression of the prayer of faith. Mental assent is one thing, but the rubber meets the road when we choose to obey His voice. Because your adversity has forced you deeper into His heart through His Word, you are more sensitive to His living voice. He will instruct you along the way. He will be your life coach — there with wisdom at every turn. He knows what you do not know and His instruction comes out of His all-knowingness.

Read the following Scriptures and let the Living Jesus speak to you. Write down what your heart hears from Him as He promises you Himself.

I will instruct you and teach you in the way you should go; I will counsel you with my loving eye on you. (Psalm 32:8)

But the eyes of the Lord are on those who fear him, on those whose hope is in his unfailing love, to deliver them from death and keep them alive in famine. (33:18)

For the eyes of the Lord range throughout the earth to strengthen those whose hearts are fully committed to him. (2 Chronicles 16:9)

PROCESSING THE PROCESS

God has no other reason for allowing your adversity into you life other than to bring good from it—a kind of good will come that can't come any other way. You can't wish your situation away or make it change. You're there. It's your current reality. Surrender to and embrace the process, or fall into resentment, petulance, and depression. It will either enrich you, or it will diminish you.

What have you decided?

Can you genuinely pray along these lines? *Father, I choose to thank You for my adversity because I know You are doing deep work that will be to my benefit and to the benefit of those I love. I don't have to see that work to know it. I surrender to Your timing and to Your ways. I know that as long as this adversity is in my life, You are using it.*

Write a prayer of surrender in your own words.

God designed prayer as a process because He uses our needs and desires as the entry points for His presence and power. It is during the process of prayer that we are drawn more deeply into relationship with Him. His Word takes on new meaning. We become desperate for Him, and we open our lives more fully to His living voice. He can speak more deeply into our lives because our lives are more open to Him.

He is a God of promise, and when He speaks, He speaks promises. When He promises, you begin to see with the eyes of your heart. You can look at what your physical eyes register and see beyond the immediate.

SEEING GOD'S WORD

Paul says this:

"I pray that the eyes of your heart may be enlightened in order that you may know *the hope to which he has called you, the riches of his glorious inheritance in his holy people, and his incomparably great power for us who believe"* (Ephesians 1:18–19; author's emphasis).

The Greek word translated "know" in this passage literally means "to see; not the mere act of seeing but the actual perception of some object; to see and understand." This particular Greek word suggests fullness of knowledge, not progressing or growing in knowledge. To know in this sense means to fully understand. God's plan is that we will see the hope, the riches, and the power. God wants to *show* you His will. He wants your inner eyes to receive light so that you will *know*.

I see! You've probably used these words to mean, "I understand fully!" God wants you to see the hope of your calling, the riches available to you and His incomparably great power for you. Jesus said to Nicodemus, "Very truly I tell you, no one can see the kingdom of God unless they are born again" (John 3:3). To state it another way, if a person is born again, he or she can see the kingdom of God. The person whom the Spirit of God indwells has the spiritual ability to see. Seeing spiritual truth changes one's perception of material facts.

Here's what I mean: Jesus suggested to Nicodemus that the Spirit is like the wind. Once again, Jesus points to an earth picture to explain a spirit truth. The wind has no substance. You don't know where it comes from or where it's going. You can't grab hold of it and feel its texture. You only know wind because of its effects.

Suppose, then, that a person decides that he does not believe in the wind. Wind, he decides, is the figment of someone's imagination. No one can prove wind. He prefers to stick to things that can be empirically proven. This person will reach some strange conclusions about what is true. For example, this person will conclude that trees lean over all by themselves sometimes or that leaves lying quietly on the ground sometimes jump up and twirl through the air. This person will ascribe power where there is no power. He will not understand that the trees and the leaves are responding to a power that is acting on them.

If a person who does not believe in the wind and a person who believes in and understands the wind look at the same scene, they will see two startlingly different truths. The first will see trees bending over; the second will see the wind.

The person who learns to observe with spirit eyes will look at earth and see Spirit. This person will understand that everything he sees on the earth is the effect of spirit. This person will know and understand the whole truth, the reality, and will not be limited to time bound, earthbound perceptions and shortsighted vision. This person, seeing the truth, will be free to live in harmony with it, no longer bound to and limited by a caricature of the truth. Jesus said, "If you hold to my teaching, you are really my disciples. Then you will know the truth, and *the truth will set you free*" (8:31–32; author's emphasis).

SEE THE KINGDOM

Jesus uses the language of "seeing" when He explains how He knew God's will while limited to His earth abilities. He said, "Very truly I tell you, the Son can do nothing by himself; he can do only what he *sees* his Father doing, because whatever the Father does, the Son also does. For the Father loves the Son and *shows* him all he does" (John 5:19–20; author's emphasis). Another time He stated, "I am telling you what I have *seen* in the Father's presence" (8:38; author's emphasis). When Jesus makes these statements, He is not talking about what He saw in His preexistent state, when He was with the Father before He came to earth. When Jesus came to earth, He took upon Himself the form of a man. In other words, He limited Himself to living in time and space. He has no access to preexistent knowledge. When He had supernatural knowledge and insight, it was because the Father had revealed it to Him and caused Him to see (understand) what was not visible to the human eye.

God gives His children spiritual vision. In order to understand how spiritual vision functions, we'll look at physical vision.

What is vision? Vision is the ability to see. What I *see* becomes what I *know*. For example, once I see the color red, I know what the color red looks like. Yet I can never know what red is without seeing it. Once I see a person's face, I know what that person looks like. I can never know it without seeing it. Everything I see becomes part of what I know.

What I see gives me direction. I have to see where I'm going in order to get to my destination. I need physical vision to navigate my physical world.

However, I don't see with my eyes. I see with my brain. My eyeballs receive the stimulus, reflected light, which is carried as electrical impulses to my brain. When the electrical impulses reach my occipital lobe, an image registers on my brain. My brain interprets it, decides on the proper response, stamps it into my memory, and processes it into everything else that I know. "Seeing" is a finished work when my brain has developed a picture and has given it what we call "meaning."

The brain's ability to see can be activated by the imagination or the memory. Your brain can picture a familiar scene or can create a scene out of random information stored in your memory bank. Your brain does not need your eyes in order to create a picture, once the picture has initially been seen. It's all in the brain. Seeing is when a picture is imprinted on your brain so that it becomes part of what you know.

If I said your spouse's name, or your child's name, or your best friend from childhood's name, you could immediately "see" his or her face. If I said, "Think about sitting at your kitchen table with a cup of coffee," you could "see" the table and the coffee cup. You see with your brain.

Vision differs from the other physical senses. To use any of the other senses, you need only two things: the stimulus and the ability to receive the stimulus. In other words, to hear you need something to hear and the ability to hear it; to taste you need something to taste and the ability to taste it. Each sense works this way — except the sense of sight. Sight requires the presence of a third element. In order to see, you need something to see, the ability to see it, and *light*.

Vision occurs when your eyes receive the light reflected off an object and send the image to your brain. Without the presence of light, vision cannot occur.

Spiritual vision works the same way. Spiritual vision occurs when God creates a picture within your mind—on your brain—of spiritual realities. In physical vision, the impetus for sight is light bouncing off physical objects. In spiritual vision, the impetus for sight is light reflected off spiritual realities. Vision cannot occur without a light source. The light source for spiritual vision is Jesus. Recall that God created light for the earth because Light existed in the eternal realms. The light we know on earth is pointing us to the Light that has always been.

The Jesus light illuminates kingdom realities. They register on my understanding and become part of what I know. Remember Paul's prayer? "I pray that the eyes of your heart may be enlightened in order that you may *know*" (Ephesians 1:18; author's emphasis).

Solid, true, authentic kingdom realities are within you. When you were born into the kingdom of God, the kingdom of God was born into you. Kingdom realities are within you and "the true light that gives light to everyone" (John 1:9), Jesus, is causing you to "see" them. They are imprinted on your brain. You understand them.

How will you know the hope to which He has called you? How will you know His riches which He has invested in you? How will you know His incomparably great power that is working for you and in you? He will give you Light. He will enlighten the eyes of your heart. Then you will know. You will see and fully perceive.

Through the steady discipline of prayer, spiritual vision is sharpened. The more we live in His presence, the more opportunity He has to enhance our ability to see and bring into sharper focus what we already see. Spiritual vision is how faith operates. "Now faith is confidence in what we hope for and *assurance* [know, perceive] of what we *do not see*" (Hebrews 11:1; author's emphasis).

DAY 4

SPIRITUAL VISION SURPASSES PHYSICAL VISION

The person with clear spiritual vision will recognize dimensions of reality that are invisible to the physical senses. In the second chapter of Luke, we are introduced to two such people.

Now there was a man in Jerusalem called Simeon, who was righteous and devout. He was waiting for the consolation of Israel, and the Holy Spirit was on him. It had been revealed to him by the Holy Spirit that he would not die before he had seen the Lord's Messiah (Luke 2:25–26).

What have we learned about Simeon so far? We know that he has no distinctive titles and holds no position of leadership. He is described merely as "a man in Jerusalem." We know that the Holy Spirit was on him. In other words, he was especially attuned to the moving of the Spirit and his life was open and available to the Spirit's leading. We know that God had placed into Simeon's life a vision — a clear mental picture of a future event. The vision is a promise from God. The Spirit had revealed to Simeon that he would not die until he had seen the Messiah. In verses 27–30 we read,

Moved by the Spirit, he went into the temple courts. When the parents brought in the child Jesus to do for him what the custom of the Law required, Simeon took him in his arms and praised God, saying: "Sovereign Lord, as you have promised, you may now dismiss your servant in peace. For my eyes have seen your salvation."

Now we see that Simeon, moving in the flow of the Spirit, went to the Temple, where he saw Mary and Joseph bringing the infant Jesus "to do for him what the custom of the Law required." Do you see what that phrase implies? Mary and Joseph were doing something ordinary — something every Jewish family did. Probably other families were doing the same thing on the same day. Many people that day looked at Mary and Joseph and the infant Jesus. Yet when Simeon looked at this ordinary, everyday scene, he saw what no one else saw. He saw the Messiah when everybody else saw a mother and a father and a baby. Others saw the appearance. Simeon saw the truth.

Next we meet a woman named Anna. In Luke 2:36–38 we learn that Anna was a prophetess. She was especially called and gifted by God to discern His activity in the world. She had spent most of her life worshipping, fasting, and praying. In prayer, she had developed an extreme sensitivity to the moving of the Spirit. Like Simeon, when she looked at the family from Nazareth, she recognized the Messiah, the Promise of God.

Nothing in the material realm identified Jesus as God's Promised One. Only those who had spiritual vision recognized Him. Those who knew the Scriptures and the Law best, the religious leaders of the day, did not recognize the truth when He stood in front of them. Jesus said they were "blind guides." Their spiritual eyes were darkened, and they did not see the Spirit. Their understanding was limited to things they could perceive with their physical senses.

You have a layer of spiritual senses that your bodily senses represent. You will always have a choice. You can look at situations from the limitations of your earthly perceptions, or you can look with the eyes of spirit. You can see the kingdom.

SPIRITUAL VISION WORKS TWO WAYS

In Simeon, we can clearly see vision working in two ways. The first way we can see vision working is in Simeon's ability to see the Spirit in an ordinary event. When he looked at earth, he saw spiritual truth—he saw the Wind. He was alert to the Spirit. He expected the promise. Spiritual vision gives the ability to discern between appearance and truth.

Second, God gave him a specific promise upon which Simeon could base his prayers. God showed Simeon through His Spirit that Simeon would see the Messiah before he died. Scripture says it had been revealed to him. This wording implies that the promise did not come in a sudden one-time encounter, but progressively took root in his understanding as he lived in the anointing of the Spirit. The idea grew in him and took on substance until he knew it with certainty. In his own mind, he could see it. It became part of what he knew.

Over and over again we see in the Scripture that God works by first implanting promise as vision. Abraham, Noah, Moses, Gideon, Paul, Jesus . . . the list goes on. God implants vision. God nurtures vision. God causes vision to become reality on the earth.

GOD IMPLANTS VISION

Vision is Spirit work. Only God can put promise in you and make it vision. Truth, when it is external, is an idea or a belief. It only becomes vision when it is within you. Like a baby grows inside a woman's body until time for it to be born onto the earth, vision grows in the spirit of a believer until the time for it to become reality on the earth.

When God brought forth on the earth His ultimate Promise, He did so by means of pregnancy and birth. Again, we can see an earthly picture that teaches a spiritual principle. God will impregnate you with vision. Vision is a specific promise from God to you. He takes what He sees for you and develops a picture of it in your mind. It develops gradually, slowly but surely becoming sharp and clear. God puts promises (vision) in us, and then births it through us.

I want you to examine two incidents reported in Scripture. One is when the angel announced to Mary that she would give birth to the Messiah. The other is when the Holy Spirit fell on the church at Pentecost. The language is parallel.

"You will conceive [*sullambano*] and give birth to a son, and you are to call him Jesus.' . . . The angel answered, 'The Holy Spirit will come on [*eperchomai*] you, and the power [*dunamis*] of the Most High will overshadow [*episkiazo*] you'" (Luke 1:31, 35).

Let me define the primary words in this passage.

- "conceive" (*sullambano*): "to conceive; to clasp; to take hold"
- "come on" (*eperchomai*): "to come upon forcefully"
- "power" (*dunamis*): "inherent power; power residing in a thing by virtue of its nature, or which a person or thing exerts and puts forth; explosive power; miraculous power"
- "overshadow" (*episkiazo*): "envelope in a haze; cast a shadow over"

Now look at the second, parallel passage: "In a few days you will be baptized with [*baptizo*] the Holy Spirit. . . . But you will receive [*lambano*] power [*dunamis*] when the Holy Spirit comes on [*eperchomai*] you; and you will be my witnesses in Jerusalem, and in all Judea and Samaria, and to the ends of the earth" (Acts 1:5, 8). "All of them were filled with [*pletho*] the Holy Spirit" (2:4).

The word for "receive," *lambano*, is the root of *sullambano*, "to conceive." The word for "baptized with" means "covered over, overwhelmed; immersed." They were "filled with" the Holy Spirit—this phrase means not only to be filled up, but also to be fulfilled or completed. Do you see the pattern?

CHURCH	MARY
Overwhelmed by the Holy Spirit	Overshadowed by the Most High
Holy Spirit fell upon them	Holy Spirit fell upon her
The power inherent in God was infused into them	The power inherent in God was infused into her
Received the Promised One (Acts 2:33)	Conceived the Promised One
Filled with Holy Spirit	Filled with Holy Spirit

This is God's pattern. This is how He works to put His promises inside you and make them vision.

PREGNANT WITH PROMISE

Vision will first appear in your life in embryonic form. Vision does not come into your life full-grown. It will need time to gestate. God initiates the vision. You will need to provide the vision with the proper conditions for maturing.

The vision needs a spirit womb. Your innermost being available to God's powerful work is the place where the vision grows. Your Spirit-filled life is the environment in which the vision develops.

When a woman finds that she is pregnant, this will often serve as the motivation to change some of her habits. It is an amazing responsibility to be housing another person in your own body. You realize that everything you physically do is having direct impact on the baby.

As it dawns on you that you are pregnant with promise through the Holy Spirit, you will start to evaluate the way you think and the emotions you foster in your mind and the attitudes you live with. Are you poisoning and stunting the vision? Someone might say to a pregnant woman, "Why aren't you drinking coffee?" She might reply, "I'm with child." Make this your new response to old attitudes: "You can't come in. I'm with promise."

The vision needs nourishment. Feed the vision the Word of God. As you fill your life with God's Word, the vision will grow stronger and healthier. It will take on clearer focus, become more substantive. The natural result of nourishing your spirit will be that the vision God has entrusted to you will mature.

Because the Word of God is living, and is being spoken to you now from the mouth of God, it is not generic or one-size-fits-all. He can speak it right to the promise He has implanted in you. He can apply it directly and specifically. Sometimes you won't even know how the Word is feeding the vision in the moment, but will only recognize it later. But you can count on God's ability to do it.

The vision has developmental stages. Be patient. God always reveals His infinite truth in finite stages. The vision will progressively unfold as you walk in obedience. Consider Abraham. Observe how his vision continued to unfold and develop.

In Genesis 12:1–4, God first implants the vision.

The Lord had said to Abram, "Go from your country, your people and your father's household to the land I will show you. I will make you into a great nation, and I will bless you; I will make your name great, and you will be a blessing. I will bless those who bless you, and whoever curses you I will curse; and all peoples on earth will be blessed through you." So Abram went, as the Lord had told him.

The vision was vague at best. Abraham is to go to a land that God will show him. God will bless him and make him into a great nation. Abraham knows no more than that. He has no clear picture of the mature plan, just an embryonic vision. But he left, as the Lord had told him.

When Abraham reaches a certain place in Canaan, the Lord appears to him. This time He was a little more specific. "To your offspring I will give this land," He said in Genesis 12:7. The vision was taking clearer shape. It had moved from "the land I will show you" to "this land."

In 13:14–17, Abraham has given the vision time and nourishment, and God fleshes it out further.

"Look around from where you are, to the north and south, to the east and west. All the land that you see I will give to you and your offspring forever. I will make your offspring like the dust of the earth, so that if anyone could count the dust, then your offspring could be counted. Go, walk through the length and breadth of the land, for I am giving it to you."

God lays out the boundaries of the land. Furthermore, He expands on His promise to make of Abraham a great nation. He clarifies that the vision is not only qualitative greatness but also numerical greatness.

Abraham has a problem—at least he thinks he does. God has given him the vision of fathering a great nation, but Abraham doesn't even have one son. Abraham expresses his concern. "Sovereign Lord, what can you give me since I remain childless and the one who will inherit my estate is Eliezer of Damascus? . . . You have given me no children; so a servant in my household will be my heir" (15:2–3). Notice how Abraham states his analysis. He says, "You *have given* me no children . . . a servant *will be* my heir" (author's emphasis). Abraham thinks it's too late. He sees only one way for God to bring the vision about: He'll have to use Abraham's servant, Eliezer of Damascus. In response, God gives Abraham more detail of the vision, a detail He had not yet stated. "This man will not be your heir, but a son who is your own flesh and blood will be your heir" (15:4). The vision continues to take on clearer form.

In 15:13–16, God fills in more details. For the first time, He tells Abraham that his descendants will be strangers in a country that will enslave them for 400 years, but afterward they will come out with great possessions. In the fourth generation, God says Abraham's descendants will return to the Promised Land. Then, God adds more specifics. He gives clearer boundaries of the land of the vision. "To your descendants I give this land, from the Wadi of Egypt to the great river, the Euphrates — the land of the Kenites, Kenizzites, Kadmonites, Hittites, Perizzites, Rephaites, Amorites, Canaanites, Girgashites and Jebusites" (v. 18). The vision has progressed from "the land I will show you" to "this land" to the detailed description above. Progressive vision. Each step of obedience opening up new dimensions, new understandings. One step makes the next step clear. Step-by-step, following the Voice that grows the vision.

Finally, God appears to Abraham when he is 99 years old. In the physical realm, Abraham still has no heir. Yet God says, "No longer will you be called Abram; your name will be Abraham, for I have made you a father of many nations" (17:5). Do you see what God said? "I *have made you* a father of many nations" (author's emphasis). Before that, God had said, "I *will make you* into a great nation" (12:2). In the spiritual realm, the work is done. The only thing left is for spiritual truth to be manifested in the material realm. In 17:6–14, God sets forth the terms of the covenant. He gives Abraham a sign of the covenant in the flesh — circumcision. He tells Abraham clearly that not only will the heir come from his own body but from the body of his wife, Sarah. He says, "But my covenant I will establish with Isaac, whom Sarah will bear to you this time next year" (17:21). Now the vision is full-term. It is ready to be born on the earth.

The vision has a due date. "For the vision is yet for the appointed time; it hastens toward the goal and it will not fail. Though it tarries, wait for it; for it will certainly come, it will not delay" (Habakkuk 2:3 NASB). This is true of all vision. There is an appointed time for it to been revealed on the earth. As with Abraham, God knows your vision's due date.

The vision is for an appointed time. God implanted it in your life at exactly the right time and He will bring it about at exactly the right time. My tendency is to try to induce labor as soon as the vision enters my life. I'm inclined to be impatient. It always looks like the right time to me. God is teaching me to wait for the due date. When the vision has reached the right developmental stage, nothing can hold it back. Until that time, nothing can bring it forth. My advice is this: don't push before it's time.

The vision is God's, not yours. You are only hosting the vision. He has placed His vision into your imagination, creativity, understanding, and desires. *He* will bring about *His* vision. "Surely, just as I have intended so it has happened, and just as I have planned so it will stand" (Isaiah 14:24).

Birthing the vision will involve labor pains. Count on it. The closer the moment of birth, the harder and faster the pains come. The time comes when you have to bear down with all your might. But not until your Birthing Coach says so.

SEEING HIS VOICE

Rabbi Abraham Isaac Kook, the first Chief Rabbi of the State of Isra'el (he was appointed before it reached statehood), writes some captivating thoughts on the odd Hebrew wording of Exodus 20:18. It follows the giving of the Ten Commandments. The English translations have cleaned it up so that it sounds more plausible. The closest translation seems to be the King James Version, which says, "And the people saw the thunderings, the lightnings, the noise of the trumpet, and the mountain smoking: and when the people saw it, they removed, and stood afar off." In the Hebrew it specifically says, "And all the people saw the sounds." Here is what Rabbi Kook says about it.

> *The Midrash* calls our attention to an amazing aspect of the Sinaitic revelation: the Jewish people were able to see what is normally only heard. What does this mean?
>
> At their source, sound and sight are united. Only in our limited, physical world, in this *"alma deperuda"* (world of separation), are these phenomena disconnected and detached. It is similar to our perception of lightning and thunder, which become increasingly separated from one another as the observer is more distanced from the source.
>
> If we are bound to the present, and can view the universe only through the temporal, material framework,

then we will always perceive this divide between sight and sound. The prophetic vision at Mount Sinai, however, granted the people the unique perspective of one standing near the source of Creation. At that level, they witnessed the underlying unity of the universe. They were capable of seeing sounds and hearing sights.

God's revelation at Sinai was registered by all their senses simultaneously, as a single, undivided perception.

In this statement in Exodus 20:18, the word translated "thunderings" in "the people saw the thunderings"—is the word for "voice." It is the same word used in the opening of Genesis 3:8 and 3:10 for God's voice when he spoke to Adam and Eve. So in Exodus 20:18, you could as easily say, "All the people saw the voice . . ."

We are closer to His voice than the Israelites at Sinai were. He is inside of us. His word is in our hearts. He is not speaking to us from a mountain, but from inside. Closer than close. You are so close to His voice that you can "see" it.

Remember that to see, you need light. The light in the kingdom is Jesus. Paul writes that the light is in "the face of Christ" (2 Corinthians 4:6). God gives us the light of His glory in the face of Jesus.

An emerging science is the study of facial communication, or what you might call "seeing the voice." Studies done on infants 18 to 20 weeks old show that, even at a preverbal age, they read facial expressions to understand speech. A thought or emotion registers on the face before it is spoken. The face registers the true emotion, even if the words are meant to mask the emotion. A highly specific science of mapping the facial muscles called facial action coding system (FACS) is a system by which you can read a person's face and know his thoughts. Even though a person can learn to quickly rearrange his face to mask emotion, the true emotion always registers on the face, even if only fleetingly.

Malcolm Gladwell wrote, in an article for the New Yorker entitled "The Naked Face," "When we experience a basic emotion, a corresponding message is automatically sent to the muscles of the face. That message may linger just a fraction of a second, or be detectable only if you attached electrical sensors to the face, but it's always there."

Look into Jesus' face. Keep your eyes fixed on His face. You will see His voice.

DAY 5

RECOGNIZING VISION

When God puts His promises in you, you will know it. You'll find that it is woven into your spiritual DNA. You can't get rid of it. You may become discouraged. You may decide one day not to believe it anymore. But you wake up the next day, and you believe it again in spite of yourself. As the vision develops, you can see how God has always been moving you toward the vision. The abilities and interests He has given you, the advantages and the disadvantages, the circumstances — both good and bad — all have been shaping the vision and preparing for its birth. Even your adversity is moving you forward.

In the process of developing the vision, God will have to take you through times and bring you to crisis points where you will recognize that you have some of your own flesh wrapped around the promise. God has to circumcise all your flesh from His vision. Be aware that it is always God's work in your life when you encounter faith challenges. His work is progressing the vision, even when it is painful. Right now, in your adversity, God is shaping the vision.

—~~—

Peace in the Midst of Pain

Author Judy Hampton shares this testimony about how her pain has shaped her, making her into someone different than she was before and bringing her into rich ministry.

We have been dealing with a prodigal son for more than 35 years. He has struggled with an addiction problem since his teens. We tried everything to bring about sobriety. Twenty-five years ago, he met a young gal and they eventually married. It appeared he had forsaken his former lifestyle, and we were thrilled at this new beginning. Eventually they had three beautiful children, and we loved and enjoyed those grands every moment we were together.

Sadly, sobriety didn't last, and soon chaos began again. After each incident, we would receive a phone call informing us that we could no longer see the grandchildren. It was during this time we learned a new word, deflection. Blame was deflected on us.

In the beginning, I thought I would die. I could hardly breathe. I collapsed into the fetal position and sobbed for hours. It was like the death of an entire family.

Weeks later, after a typically sleepless night, I dragged myself downstairs to the family room and turned on the TV. I quickly discovered there is nothing on TV at 2:00 a.m. Looking back I can see that God was bringing me to the end of myself so He could transform my life.

I'd been in Bible studies for years, but I'd never read the Bible to personally hear from God . . . until that morning. I dug it out and it randomly opened to the Book of Psalms. Imagine my astonishment as my eyes fell on Psalm 34:18, "The Lord is close to the brokenhearted and saves those who are crushed in spirit." Those words jumped off the page and ministered to my hurting heart. It whet my appetite, and I kept reading for hours. As a result of this deep adversity, a paradigm shift took place in my relationship with Him. In the ensuing months, I had no problem getting up earlier and earlier. I was hungry to hear from God. He was changing me from the inside out.

One morning I laid face down on the carpet in our family room and wept as I surrendered our son and those precious grandchildren over to God. Instantly I was flooded with peace. Peace that cannot be explained, only received.

The family adversity went for years, and so did those phone calls. We were allowed to see the grandchildren until another crisis ensued. Then ten years ago there was a scandal and they moved out of town in the middle of the night. We have never seen our grandchildren since.

However, my response was totally different. You see, "I would have despaired unless I had believed that I would see the goodness of the Lord in the land of the living" *(27:13 NASB).*

His goodness has allowed my pain to be used as a platform to minister to thousands of brokenhearted moms across the country. Using grandchildren as emotional blackmail has become an epidemic in a country filled with narcissists. I meet moms gripped by the same kind of grief I experienced. I understand.

My counsel is always the same. Get into His Word, saturate yourself in it, hide it in your heart, and draw your life from Him. He is able — more than able — to accomplish whatever concerns us.

I am learning that there is absolutely nothing wrong with loving and adoring our grandchildren, but when I compare that to experiencing peace in the midst of pain, I realize it is just overflow.

—w—

Judy sees her adversity in a new light. She finds the great joy of ministering in the power that comes out of deep pain.

—w—

The Aha of God's Grace

As a relationship coach, certified Christian life coach, and director of women's ministries in a large church in Texas, Linda Goldfarb has deep impact on many lives. With all her training and experience in her field, her most important credentials come in the form of real-life faith challenges. She tells this story that she describes as "moving from adversity into the aha grace of God."

Shawn entered college on a spiritual high. He had just experienced sharing the gospel of Christ with a young man at youth camp, "Mom, Jesus used me in a mighty way this weekend. Jeremy accepted Him as his Savior!" These words filled me with contagious but short-lived joy.

"Mom, there may be a god, but I don't know if my god is your God." After two months of college, these were the first words Shawn

spoke into me. Emotions of betrayal, devastation, fear, outrage, and confusion swirled like an unending tornado in my mind, bursting from my lungs in cries and sobs of unharnessed disbelief.

The world was consuming my firstborn son, and I felt helpless to save him. Yet, hope remained in the form of prayer from intercessors. Daily prayer expanded into weeks, months, and years. No matter how far Shawn strayed, prayer kept him near to my mind and closer still to my heart.

My heart was heavy with a recent negative conversation I had with my oldest daughter when the phone rang and Shawn's upbeat voice on the other end of the phone caught me slightly off-guard. As I shared pleasantries, he knew something was wrong. "Heather's making some poor choices, and I'm afraid of what might happen."

"You can't choose her fire, Mom." Shawn's voice rang with a spiritual truth I'd never heard from him before.

"God has fire for each of us, Mom. You can't choose what Heather or I have to go through. It's God's fire, not yours."

Shawn's words have been repeated hundreds of times over the years into the hearts of parents I coach. Today, Shawn and his wife, Betty, are active members of their church, raising four children to love and honor Jesus Christ.

While I was in my fire those many years ago, I didn't see what God was doing. The pain of losing Shawn to the world was nearly unbearable. But looking back everything is made clear; I couldn't choose his fire. God had Shawn exactly where He needed him to be in order to remove the dross holding him back from being the follower of Christ he is today. All He needed me to do was let go and trust Him.

—m—

THE PURPOSE OF SPIRITUAL VISION

Why does God do His work through vision? Why engage humans before the fact? Why not just let His work show up on earth unannounced? God says, "See, the former things have taken place, and new things I declare; before they spring into being I announce them to you" (Isaiah

42:9). He announces His intentions into our desires or understanding. Then, He brings His intentions into being in response to our prayers. Why?

In Isaiah 48:3–6 we read,

I foretold the former things long ago, my mouth announced them and I made them known; then suddenly I acted, and they came to pass. For I knew how stubborn you were; your neck muscles were iron, your forehead was bronze. Therefore I told you these things long ago; before they happened I announced them to you so that you could not say, "My images brought them about; my wooden image and metal god ordained them."

In other words, God will announce His plans before He brings them into being so that we will recognize His work and will not attribute His power to anyone or anything else.

Jesus said, "I have told you now before it happens, so that when it does happen, you will believe" (John 14:29). When you see the picture inside you take shape on the earth, you will recognize the work of the One who has the power to do what He has promised (Romans 4:21).

God gives impossible vision. If it were possible, it would be an assignment or a project—but it is vision. When vision takes shape on the earth, there will be no doubt about whose vision it is. God will implant vision in you that only He can bring into being. "We have these treasures in jars of clay to show that this all-surpassing power is from God and not from us" (2 Corinthians 4:7).

If you have scaled back or watered down God's vision, you are not "[taking] hold of that for which Christ Jesus took hold of [you]" (Philippians 3:12). God will not bring about a diluted form of His vision. You may bring about a diluted form of His vision, but He will not. Abraham and Sarah took it upon themselves to bring God's vision into being, and Ishmael was the result. Moses tried to bring about God's vision for freeing his people in the power of his own flesh. He freed one slave from one taskmaster for one day.

If what you envision about a situation negates or underestimates the power of God, you are not praying the vision, not claiming the promise. You are limiting God by expecting of Him only what you can imagine. In your adversity, what is the Father showing you? Your marriage is struggling. What do you see in your Father's presence? Your child has strayed from his relationship with the Lord. What do you see in your Father's presence? You are struggling financially. What do you see in your Father's presence? Whatever you are facing, what do you see in your Father's presence?

A WARNING

Let me interject a warning and a clarification here. I don't want you to confuse what I'm saying with some of the concepts of visualizing or imaging so prevalent in New Age religions, or with some of the variations on the truth that have even made their way into the church. New Age concepts say that by visualizing or imaging what you want, you can make it happen. In this thought, the vision originates with you, and you, by deliberately and consistently imaging what you desire, create that reality. This is not what the Scriptures teach about how God implants His vision. A variation on that lie sometimes shows up in the church. The thinking goes that by envisioning what you want God to do, you will cause God to do it and you will create the "energy" or the "power" to bring it to pass. Again, the distorted version of the truth puts the emphasis on your flesh. This is not what Scripture teaches about how God implants His vision.

The most effective lies are those that are close to the truth. Be careful and do not blur the crisp edges of the truth. God gives you the mental picture of His reality — the reality that exists in the heavenly realms and is available to be manifested in the earth. The picture He gives you is so that you can have confidence when things seem discouraging. It is also so that when He creates on the earth the reality He has already shown you, you will recognize His hand at work.

What do you see in the presence of your Father?

Is He causing you to view your adversity differently?

WEEK 3

THE PROMISE OF PRAYER

The promise of prayer is a transformed heart. Through the ongoing discipline of prayer, we are brought into direct and intimate contact with the Father's heart. As we continually behold His glory, we are changed into His image. Our lives begin to reflect Him; our desires begin to reflect His desires. As He has constant access to us, He realigns our vision, recreates our desires, reproduces His heart. Powerful, earth-changing prayer begins in the heart of God and flows through the hearts of His people. The promise of prayer is a heart that matches His.

— LIVE A PRAYING LIFE®: OPEN YOUR LIFE TO HIS POWER AND PROVISION

DAY 1

As you let your adversity do its intended work, and you release your best ideas to His vision, you are being transformed into His image from one degree of glory to the next because you have a clearer view of His face and are more attuned to His voice. "And we all, who with unveiled faces contemplate the Lord's glory, are being transformed into his image with ever-increasing glory, which comes from the Lord, who is the Spirit" (2 Corinthians 3:18). This is your calling and your destiny, however it is being worked out. This is what brings you to completion, and brings deep, abiding satisfaction into your life.

From this passage, answer the following questions:

And we know that in all things God works for the good of those who love him, who have been called according to his purpose. For those God foreknew he also predestined to be conformed to the image of his Son, that he might be the firstborn among many brothers and sisters. And those he predestined, he also called; those he called, he also justified; those he justified, he also glorified. (Romans 8:28–30)

Do you choose to believe that God is working all the details of your adversity out toward a good end?

Do you believe that God has in mind the good of every person affected by the situation in your life right now?

Can you trust those you love to His purposes, even when there is pain along the way?

Since you were destined—designed and called—to be conformed into the image of Jesus, would any other pursuit bring satisfaction?

Let the Father show you His vision for your life—to be glorified. To be glorified means to be His outshining—His expression in the world.

ALL FOR GOOD

In our adversity, it is easier to process the pain and its outcome for our own lives than it is to see those we love in pain. But that is part of the promise of prayer. Not only is God working on your behalf and conforming you in ways that will enrich your life, but the same is also true for your children, your spouse, and your loved ones whose lives are affected by your current adversity.

When my husband passed away in 2005, my sons were in their early and mid-20s. The hardest thing was to let them grieve. Their pain caused me more pain than any other aspect of my husband's death. My youngest son was having the hardest time. Then, on top of his grief, the year that followed was a year of other disappointments and challenges for him. I was consumed with his pain. I prayed constantly for relief for him, and instead of relief, he had even more hurts.

One day the Lord presented a picture to my mind. I imagined a tableau of how my prayers for my son looked. I saw myself with my son tucked behind me and with me looking up to God and saying, "Don't hurt him!" The Lord seemed gently to whisper, "Look where you are. Right between Me and him. What if, when you feel the pain for your son, instead of crying out for Me to change his circumstances, you just bow at My feet? Look what happens. I get face-to-face with him."

I spent a lot of time bowed. But that vision God planted in me showed me that He would deal with my son's pain and that He would use it for good. All these years later, I can see what God built into his life in the midst of his pain. Joseph's explanation of why he named his second son Ephraim—which sounds like the Hebrew word for "twice fruitful"—is this: "It is because God has made me fruitful in the land of my suffering" (Genesis 41:52). I am Ephraim, and so are my sons. Fruitful in the land of our suffering.

In your adversity, is it easier for you to accept God's work and ways in your life than in the lives of loved ones? Write down the names of those you love whose pain you are struggling with.

Beside each name, write *Ephraim*. Let it be your bowing down. Embrace the vision God presents to your heart and mind.

A LESSON IN BURDEN BEARING

"My burden is light" (Matthew 11:30). This is one of Jesus' more paradoxical statements. He makes it in the form of a promise. He doesn't promise you will have no burdens but that His burden is light. How can that be? Isn't the factor that defines something as a burden is that it is heavy?

This promise comes on the heels of an invitation from Rabbi Jesus to take His yoke. This was the way a rabbi described a disciple putting himself under that rabbi's particular school of thought. Jesus said that when we take Him as our teacher, we will find rest. Not new burdensome rules, but rest—that even our burdens would be light.

It begs the question: what makes a burden heavy? In the physical realm—God's illustration of spiritual truth—what makes something heavy is gravity. The downward gravitational pull of the earth makes something heavy.

Imagine with me now that I am about to pick up a huge, heavy boulder. Can you see the scene? I struggle to pick it up and put it on my back. It's too heavy for me. It crushes me to the ground. I am paralyzed under its weight. Got it?

Reset the scene. I'm about to pick up exactly the same boulder. Nothing has changed about the burden. Except that this time when I pick it up, I'm on Mars. Since gravity on Mars is so significantly less that it is negligible, the very same burden that paralyzed me on Earth is light as a feather on Mars. The difference is not in the burden but in the environment in which we carry the burden. When we try to carry it in our flesh, it crushes us. When we carry it in the Spirit, it is light.

We may have to transfer out of flesh to the Spirit hundreds of times a day. But one day we'll get into the spiritual realm with that burden and stay there. The burden may not change immediately, but our reaction to it will. We can hold it up to the Lord instead of having it weigh us down and paralyze us.

Don't slip into guilt or condemnation here. The Lord is on your side. He is not scolding you. He is inviting you. Let Him show you how to transfer the burden. A Scripture He gives you to use? A phrase? A mental picture? Just ask Him.

FUELED BY FAITH OR FUELED BY FLESH?

Seeing the promises of prayer become real in your experience requires faith and obedience. As it turns out, faith and obedience are the same thing. We express faith by exercising obedience.

Faith and prayer are inseparable. Faith fuels prayer. Prayer expresses faith. The two are intertwined. One does not exist without the other. But what is faith? Is faith a feeling that can be worked up? Is faith feeling sure that we know what God will do? Does faith have anything to do with feeling? It is very important that we look closely at faith because a misguided understanding of faith and how it operates has caused many pray-ers to lose heart.

THE MIDWIFE OF VISION

How does vision become reality on the earth? How does the picture God has placed within you take shape in the material realm?

"The promise [vision] comes [is translated into the material realm] by faith" (Romans 4:16). Faith is the midwife of vision. Examine this statement that Paul made in the Book of Romans:

"The promise comes..." *Comes from where to where? From heaven to earth.*

"The promise comes..." *How? What is the avenue that brings the promise from heaven to earth?*

"The promise comes by faith." *Faith brings the promise out of heaven and makes it reality on the earth.*

When God puts promise in you, faith is the process by which that promise is realized in the circumstances of earth. The promise comes by faith.

What gave life to the promise? The voice of God. The voice of God that framed the worlds in the beginning is the same voice that frames your world by means of His promises. God speaks the promise into your heart—lifts it off the pages of Scripture and burrows it into your heart. There it finds life.

Recall the Scripture portions we examined to see the process of being impregnated with promise. God overshadowed Mary and spoke the Word into her womb. Mary conceived. The word means, "to take hold of." "And Mary said, 'Behold, the bondslave of the Lord; may it be done to me according to your word'" (Luke 1:38 NASB). Mary received the word of God. She let it take up residence in her. She let it abide in her (John 15:7) and dwell in her richly (Colossians 3:16).

When the Israelites left Egypt, they left with a promise. God had a land ready for them to inhabit. The generation that left Egypt never entered the Promised Land. Why? The writer of Hebrews explains: "For we also have had the good news proclaimed to us, just as they did; but the message they heard was of no value to them, because they did not *share the faith* of those who obeyed" (Hebrews 4:2; author's emphasis). Even though they were told about the good news of God's provision for them, it did them no good. For them, there might as well not have been a Promised Land. They lived as if no Promised Land existed. Because they did not mix the word of God with faith. The word translated "share" is a word that means "to unite one thing with another; to cause several parts to combine into an organic structure."

For example, consider the difference between a mixture and a solution. In a mixture, several elements are put together, but each retains its original form and can be separated out again. Fruit salad is a mixture. In a solution, the molecules of the elements combine to make an entirely new substance. When salt and water are united, their molecules combine. The salt is dissolved in the water. A whole new substance with a whole new molecular structure results. That is the sense of the Greek word *sugkerannumi,* translated "share."

Just as in physical conception the father's sperm must unite with the mother's egg, when God speaks promise into your spirit womb, it has to be combined with faith in order for conception to occur. Just as the new life that begins in that moment of physical conception must attach itself to the mother's womb, the vision that is conceived must find a foothold and take root in your mind. It must adhere to your innermost being and be immovable and steadfast.

So now we wrestle with that fundamental question, what is faith? How does faith function?

FAITH WORKS

It makes sense to me that if you observe how something functions, you then discover its definition. So, by observing faith in operation, I reach the conclusion that faith's central definition — its root definition — is obedience to the present-tense voice of the Lord. Though nothing is earned, and though all comes through grace, that does not negate response on our part. Freely offered salvation must be actively received. Freely offered promises of God's provision must be actively received into our lives. Paul says that God's grace toward him was "not without effect. No, I worked harder than all of them—yet not I, but the grace of God that was with me" (1 Corinthians 15:10).

As I explained in the first edition of *Live a Praying Life*, Hebrews 11:3 is the thesis statement for this whole treatise on faith: "By faith we understand that the universe was formed at God's command, so that what is seen was not made out of what was visible."

From this statement, the writer begins to document his case. Faith, he is saying, is when the invisible power of God's Word—that is His *rhema*, His present-tense word—produces a visible effect on the earth.

Now read through verses 4–40. How does the Scripture define faith?

- "By faith Abel brought God a better offering" (v. 4).
- "By faith Noah . . . built an ark" (v. 7).
- "By faith Abraham . . . obeyed and went" (v. 8).
- "By faith Abraham . . . offered Isaac as a sacrifice" (v. 17).
- "By faith Isaac blessed Jacob and Esau" (v. 20).

On and on it goes. These people who are held up as examples of faith were commended for what they did—not felt—in response to God's voice. What defined the action as "faith"? It was an action taken because God said to take it!

When God spoke and a human acted on what He said, His power became visible on the earth. The invisible became visible through the faith responses of humans.

Examine the eternal record—the Scripture—for a consistent pattern of how the Word of God moved from invisible to visible through actions that were fueled by faith. The writer of Hebrews states: "We do not want you to become lazy, but to imitate those who through faith and patience inherit what has been promised" (Hebrews 6:12). We are to examine the lives of those who exhibited faith so that we can imitate them. We can't look at every example the Scripture gives, so we will look at some representative examples.

In Exodus 7:1–6, the drama unfolds.

Then the Lord said to Moses, "See, I have made you like God to Pharaoh, and your brother Aaron will be your prophet. You are to say everything I command you, and your brother Aaron is to tell Pharaoh to let the Israelites go out of his country. But I will harden Pharaoh's heart, and though I multiply my signs and wonders in Egypt, he will not listen to you. Then I will lay my hand on Egypt and with mighty acts of judgment I will bring out my divisions, my people the Israelites. And the Egyptians will know that I am the Lord when I stretch out my hand against Egypt and bring the Israelites out of it." Moses and Aaron did just as the Lord commanded them *(author's emphasis).*

Before the narrative opens, describing each of the encounters between Pharaoh and Moses and Aaron, do you see that God is announcing what He has available? He is describing the power and provision that He has at the ready. He assures them upfront that even when things look discouraging, all is going according to His plan. No matter what Moses and Aaron see, they can be sure that God is in charge. He impregnates them with promise. He paints a picture in their minds of what they can ultimately expect.

Notice, too, that an essential element of His plan is what Moses and Aaron will do in response to His voice. Now read the familiar story, but read it with new eyes. Find it in Exodus 6–11, then skip to Exodus 12:29–36. Maybe you will want to use your Bible computer software or a Bible website and copy and paste these sections in a word-processing program so you can print it out and scribble all over it. Look for the following points.

At what point in each encounter did Moses and Aaron know what God wanted them to do? Did God tell them obedience by obedience, in the moment? Or did He lay out His whole plan in detail from the beginning?

Underline every time you see the phrase, "just as the LORD commanded." How did Moses and Aaron decide what to do or say at each encounter with Pharaoh?

In each encounter, notice that Moses and Aaron were to say something and to do something. If you have printed out the passages, draw an arrow to each phrase and label it *Say* or *Do*. Just for fun, write it in a new color.

In each encounter, did God's power come into the environment of earth before or after Moses and Aaron obeyed, both in word and deed? Mark the phrases that tell you there was cause and effect between Moses and Aaron's obedience and the visible demonstration of God's power.

As you look at each encounter, consider this: If Moses and Aaron did not have a picture to look at on the inside of them, what would the circumstances on the outside have looked like? Based on the observable facts—the empirical evidence—how might they have interpreted the outcome of each encounter? Beside the description of each encounter, write something that you will understand, such as *good* or *bad*. Or draw a smiling face or a frowning face.

Identify the instances where there seemed to be progress, then things reversed and Moses and Aaron must have been disappointed. Write some identifying mark or word by those incidents.

Identify all the times that Moses' enemy tried to placate him by suggesting a compromise — a partial obedience.

In the end, did God bring about exactly the vision He had put inside Moses and Aaron?

DAY 2

IMITATE THE FAITHFUL: MOSES AND AARON

What can we learn about how faith functions from this pivotal event in the Israel's history?

Faith begins with the voice of God. He impregnates you with promise, giving you certainty about what He wants to do, but not how He will do it. Your job is to obey moment by moment. Say what He tells you to say and do what He tells you to do. God has designed faith to work this way. This moment-by-moment following will require you to form a desperate dependence on God, clinging to Him and looking to Him every second.

Often we are unsettled by not knowing what the step after this step will be. We may be anxious when we can only see the step in front of us. But that is by deliberate design. Recently I was driving on an unfamiliar and poorly lit road at night in a dense fog. I could only see the road a few feet in front of me. My only hope was to keep moving in the light I had, knowing that as I moved the light would reveal the next little patch of road. The only way to know what the next step would be was to take the step in front of me. Every now and then, another car would be in front of me. Then I could see the patch my lights illuminated and a little bit of the patch his lights illuminated. When someone was in front of me, I could "imitate" him and see a little more. But even then, the only option was to keep moving. As I drove through the fog, the situation forced me to be alert and focused, when usually my mind would be wandering to a thousand other things.

This is exactly how God has engineered faith to work.

Faith forces you to move forward, and you can only know that it is forward because God says it is. When I was driving in my fog, because my perspective was narrowed to what I could see in front of me, I often felt as if I were going backward. As you move in faith, forward might sometimes *feel* backward. Moses and Aaron had several instances during their obedience when it appeared that things took a turn for the worse. But they knew they were going *toward* the vision.

Faith is expressed in obedience. Each time that Moses and Aaron obeyed God's voice, their act of faith released the invisible word of God to become visible on the earth. For example:

The LORD *said to Moses and Aaron, "When Pharaoh says to you, 'Perform a miracle,' then say to Aaron, 'Take your staff and throw it down before Pharaoh,' and it will become a snake." So Moses and Aaron went to Pharaoh and did just as the* LORD *commanded. Aaron threw his staff down in front of Pharaoh and his officials, and it became a snake* (Exodus 7:8–10; author's emphasis).

After the obedience, the manifestation of the promise. Always the pattern.

Faith has an enemy. Your enemy is continually working against your faith, but he can only defeat you if he can discourage you. He is not in charge. Pharaoh thought he was in charge, but it is clear from the beginning that he was not.

It's not that you are growing in faith, as we often say but that faith is growing in you. Your enemy is part of God's plan for growing faith in you. Everything your enemy tries can backfire on him and can deepen and strengthen your faith. That's what God uses him for.

As the confrontations between Moses and Aaron and the Pharaoh progress, you can see the progressive weakening of their enemy as Moses and Aaron refused to give ground. In fact, his failure was put on display so that he was proven false and weak in the eyes of both his subjects and God's people.

The ten plagues that God brought upon the enemy's territory were His plan from the outset. He fully intended that each of the ten plagues would occur because each had a special focus in the enemy's camp. Let's look at them and see how faith stands firm until the enemy is fully exposed and deposed.

The first thing to notice is that the series of plagues begins and ends with blood. The first plague is the turning of the Nile and all water into blood. The last is the blood of the lamb on the doorposts of the houses of the Israelites. Blood is the opening blow, from which the enemy never quite recovers his equilibrium, and blood is the final knockout punch. The blood frames the battle, sets the parameters, and draws the line. The enemy does not recognize that at the first appearance of the blood, his defeat is sure.

God's opening plague—turning the Nile River into blood—is a direct frontal assault on the very person of the enemy, establishing from the beginning who is God and who is not. The Nile was absolutely essential to the nation of Egypt. Everything depended on the Nile. They worshipped the Nile, and the Pharaoh was believed to be the personification of the Nile—the Nile made flesh, you might say.

Each plague directly addresses one of Egypt's deities. The Egyptians had gods and goddesses for every aspect of their daily lives. Each plague showed God to be able to overpower every god of the Egyptians. The Egyptian gods, the people believed, were especially empowered as magicians. You notice that the magicians of Egypt were able to mimic the first plagues, but not completely reproduce them. For example, they could turn the water red, but they could not undo what they had done. They could call out frogs, but they could not call them back. Quickly, the power of God outpaced the skills of the magicians.

You need to know that God and your enemy are not in a fair fight. God is not picking on someone His own size. In the first round, the enemy is knocked senseless, even though he may not go down until after a few more punches.

As your vision is gestating, God will be taking on each stronghold that the enemy has in your life. His battle plan includes calling the enemy out from his hiding places, those cubbyholes where you have tucked away little idols. God wants to prove to you that He is able to add to your life what your idols promise but cannot deliver.

Don't let your enemy convince you that he has power over you. He does not. He only has the illusion of power. He postures and lies and deceives. He wants to entice you or bully you out of the realm of faith into the realm of fear and feelings. He wants to convince you to compromise — to obey, sort of. To half obey.

Your enemy needs to hear your voice. God commanded Moses and Aaron to speak the word of the Lord to the enemy. I don't mean that you have to say words out loud, although it is not a bad idea when appropriate. Your thoughts are words and your enemy speaks in thoughts. And I don't necessarily mean that you have to address your words at the enemy. Declare in positive, declarative sentences what the Lord has promised you. It scares the enemy and it feeds your faith. Speak the word that God has put in your mouth and send those living, active sound waves into the spiritual realm where they cause reality to take on substance in the material realm.

The outcome is not in question. God declares the end from the beginning. When you are pregnant with promise, keep taking the picture that God has put in your mind out and looking at it. He creates in you an understanding of circumstances in your life from His perspective. You can learn to look at the situation as it is on earth and see the situation as it will be when brought into contact with God's power.

Review the points gleaned from Moses and Aaron's faith. Let each settle in, and let the Spirit apply it to your current adversity. Write your thoughts beside each.

• Faith begins with the voice of God.

• Faith forces you to move forward.

• Faith is expressed in obedience.

• Faith has an enemy.

• Your enemy needs to hear your voice.

• The outcome is not in question.

THE ARTIST

Earth perspective gives only a vague outline, affords only a linear perspective. The earth point of view is like an artist's *ébauche*. An ébauche is the initial underpainting that establishes the broad lines of emphasis in a projected painting. It is unfinished. It is a rough outline only meant to establish the painting's basic components. The ébauche is never meant to be the finished work. If you were to mistake an artist's ébauche for his finished work, you would misjudge his talent. If you did not wait for the mature, finished work—if you walked away having seen only the ébauche—you would never truly see the painting. The finished work exists in the mind of the artist.

When you are using your spiritual vision, God will show you the finished work before it becomes available on the earth. It is already finished in His mind. Your spirit eyes will see it before your earth eyes do. You will distinguish between an ébauche and a finished work of art. The circumstances on the earth are only the outline, alerting you to areas where God is going to complete the picture with His power.

You will see this principle laid out in the story of Jehoshaphat found in 2 Chronicles 20:1–30. Open your Bible, or print out the passage for study.

Identify the opening verses, 1–2, the situation as it appeared from the earth — the ébauche.

Underline the phrase that opens this account, "after this." After what? What preceded the enemy's attack?

How did Jehoshaphat interpret the ébauche? Did he embrace it as the finished picture? How did he react to the facts on the ground? (vv. 3–13)

As Jehoshaphat speaks truth and lines his thinking up with reality, what does he conclude? "We do not know what to do, but _____

_____

_____."

Why did Jehoshaphat fix his eyes upon God? Did he have confidence that God knew what he did not know?

Read verses 14–17. Was God's answer to Jehoshaphat's question general? Or was it specific and detailed and present-tense?

God's answer to Jehoshaphat included directions about how Jehoshaphat was to proceed and what Jehoshaphat could confidently expect from God. God's power and provision would be released by Jehoshaphat's faith response. Identify what God commanded Jehoshaphat and what God promised Jehoshaphat.

Review the ébauche as presented in the first two verses. Now observe how the view changes as God paints His picture and impregnates Jehoshaphat with promise. (vv. 15–17)

At what point did Jehoshaphat embrace the Lord's vision? After he had seen it in the material realm, or while it was still invisible? (vv. 20–21)

Read how the promise looked when it became visible on the earth. Did it match the picture God had painted in Jehoshaphat's mind? (vv. 22–27)

What was the response of Jehoshaphat and his people to seeing the picture they held in their minds take shape on the earth? What was the response of the enemy to the mighty work of God on behalf of His people? (vv. 27–30)

DAY 3

IMITATE THE FAITHFUL: JEHOSHAPHAT

What can we learn about how faith functions from this event in the life of Jehoshaphat?

At times, God forces faith out of hiding by means of sudden situations. Jehoshaphat was not anticipating the attack that was looming on his horizon. Yet God had allowed the event in order to put His power on display and to cause faith to grow in His people.

In 2 Chronicles 20:1–2, Scripture first defines the earth view of Judah's situation, the ébauche.

The Moabites and Ammonites with some of the Meunites came to wage war against Jehoshaphat. Some people came and told Jehoshaphat, "A vast army is coming against you from Edom, from the other side of the Dead Sea. It is already in Hazezon Tamar."

Jehoshaphat, however, understood that this dire description of the facts did not constitute the whole of reality. "Jehoshaphat resolved to inquire of the Lord, and he proclaimed a fast for all Judah" (v. 3). Jehoshaphat was "alarmed," but that alarm pushed him to seek God. He inquired of the Lord rather than taking the facts at face value. He inquired of the Lord because He knew God had something to impart to him that would give him direction.

When we seek Him, He reminds us of His promises, speaking them to us in the present tense. God began to fill Jehoshaphat's mind with His greatness. "Lord, the God of our ancestors, are you not the God who is in heaven? You rule over all the kingdoms of the nations. Power and might are in your hand, and no one can withstand you" (v. 6).

I know it might sound as if Jehoshaphat is reminding God, but really, God is reminding Jehoshaphat. God fills our minds with His word so naturally that if feels as if we are saying it to Him, when in reality He is saying it to us. Sometimes, the listening comes in the speaking. You begin to express prayer and find that you spontaneously speak words that you had not consciously considered before, and you actually experience new insight as you hear your own prayer.

That very kind of thing happened to me recently. My three faithful intercessors—JoAnne, Wanda, and Mary—pray for me and pray for the ministry. One day, I was telling them about an obedience to which God had clearly called me that would involve a change of habit. I was saying that in the abstract, it sounded fairly simple, but when the first opportunity arose to obey, I found it hard. It had made me recognize that something had more foothold in me than I knew. As we prayed, I was thanking God for His call to this obedience and for revealing to me that I had little idols tucked away in cubbyholes in my heart. I had never thought the word *cubbyholes* before, nor had I thought the word *idols* in terms of my experience until I was praying and that was how I was picturing it. Wanda said, "Oh, that is just what I was thinking because I'm reading *The Key: How to Let Go and Let God* by Nancy Missler, and it says that the priests in the Temple had little cubbyholes outside the Temple where they hid their idols." It was such confirmation that God is actively directing our thoughts in harmony with His and we loved it.

Faith is awakened by God voicing His Word. He was speaking His Word to Jehoshaphat, and Jehoshaphat was releasing it into the situation through prayer.

God's speaking brings the vision into focus. With every statement God's Spirit prompted in Jehoshaphat, his spiritual vision sharpened. He began to see the situation as it *would be.* God announced it to him through the mouth of the prophet Jahaziel:

Do not be afraid or discouraged because of this vast army. For the battle is not yours, but God's. Tomorrow march down against them. . . . You will not have to fight this battle. Take up your positions; stand firm and see the deliverance the LORD will give you" (vv. 15–17).

Before this picture was finished on earth, it was finished in the spiritual realm. The situation on earth merely laid out the broad lines of emphasis where the power of God would be directly applied. The earth's circumstances just set the stage for the promise. Spiritual vision enables you to see that what God has promised He is bringing to pass. He "calls into being things that were not" (Romans 4:17).

The enemy's attacks serve God's purposes. Because the assault of the enemy provided a platform for God's power, God had the opportunity to display His power and provision in a manner that would cause faith to grow in Jehoshaphat. If we never get to see God bring the finished painting out of the heavens and display it on the earth, then we won't learn to recognize an ébauche when we see one. We'll keep mistaking the ébauche for the painting.

Faith is obedience to the present voice of the Lord, and sometimes the obedience is in not acting. God does not want your flesh in action. When Jehoshaphat obeyed the Lord's command not to attack but instead to stand still and see the Lord work, all the power and provision of God flowed into the circumstances of earth.

Go through the points gleaned from Jehoshaphat's faith. Let each settle in, and let the Spirit apply it to your current adversity. Write your thoughts beside each.

At times, God forces faith out of hiding by means of sudden situations.

When we seek Him, He reminds us of His promises, speaking them to us in the present tense.

God's speaking brings the vision into focus.

The enemy's attacks serve God's purposes.

Faith is obedience to the present voice of the Lord, and sometimes the obedience is in not acting.

FAITH ON PARADE

"By faith we understand that the universe was formed at God's command, so that what is seen was not made out of what was visible" (Hebrews 11:3).

Let me review what Hebrews 11:3 tells us. The material realm was made out of God's *rhema*. When God spoke, spiritual reality took on physical form. It became substance. This activity is the first, and therefore the primary, revelation of God—who He is and how He works. Every subsequent revelation builds on this foundation.

The Old Testament faithful are put on display as real-life lessons in how the faith principle operates. When God spoke, they acted in response to His voice, and God's power and provision flowed into the circumstances of earth and became visible.

Faith is more than how you deal with certain promises. It is a continual interaction with the spiritual realm. "My righteous one will *live* by faith" (10:38; author's emphasis). Faith is not a feeling you are required to stir up. Faith is not a static attendance to a set of theological beliefs. Faith is not something you get out and dust off when you want something from God. Faith is a way of living. Until it becomes a way of living, it will not be effective. *Faith is obeying the present-tense voice of the Father.* Faith is not just *believing something.* Faith is *believing Someone.*

As you boldly obey the present-tense voice of the Father, you access His power and provision. As you live the life to which you were born, you live in your inheritance. "Now if we are children, then we are heirs — heirs of God and co-heirs with Christ" (Romans 8:17).

When faith is exercised on the earth, the power of God is released into the situation.

The writer of Hebrews says that the ancients were commended for their faith. It really means that they are witnesses to the reality of God's promise. Their experience attests to the certainty that faith in operation will access the promise. The promise comes by faith. If you want proof, look at the forefathers listed in Hebrews 11. In each of their experiences, faith was awakened by the voice of God, it was expressed through obedience to the present voice, and it resulted in the promise of God manifested in the circumstances of earth. God impregnated His people with promise, grew it in them as vision, and brought it through them as power and provision.

In fact, most of Hebrews 11 is about how faith looks in the lives of real people. Open your Bible to this chapter, or print it out and start marking it up. As you go through it, mark the verbs — the action words — that faith produced. Let's take a more detailed look at some of the instances God highlights as prime examples of how faith looks and see if the pattern holds and the definition applies.

"By faith Abel brought God a better offering than Cain did" (v. 4). How did Abel know what sacrifice would please God? He knew because God told him. If faith is what fueled Abel's action, then where did his faith come from? Faith comes only one way: "So faith comes from hearing, and hearing by the word [*rhema*] of Christ" (Romans 10:17 NASB).

Abel acted on what God told him. His obedience was called faith.

"By faith Enoch was taken from this life, so that he did not experience death" (v. 5). The author's argument is this: the Scripture testifies that Enoch walked with God so closely that his move from time into eternity required that his body simply change its form. One breath on earth, the next in eternity. Before he was taken, Enoch was "commended"—pointed out, highlighted—"as one who pleased God." Without faith, reasons the author, it is not possible to please God. God does not want your best efforts or your well-meaning actions. He wants your obedience to His voice. Since one cannot please God without faith, and since Enoch pleased God, then Enoch's life and its translation into eternity evidenced his faith.

If you are bored by word study, skip this paragraph! A side note on Enoch: The Greek word *methistemi* translated "taken"—or in the King James Version, "translated"—is the same Greek word used in Colossians 1:13. "For he has rescued us from the dominion of darkness and brought us [*methistemi*] into the kingdom of the Son he loves" (Colossians 1:13). This Greek word is interpreting a Hebrew word, which among other defi-nitions, can mean "to remove boundaries." The word used in the King James Version, *translate*, expresses the sense well. The word *translate* is from the Latin *trans* (across) and *latus* (to carry)—to carry across. When you translate a word from one language to another, you carry it across boundaries. That is what God did with Enoch. He removed the boundar-ies of earth from his body. That is what God has already done for your sprit. He has translated you into the kingdom and the life you live in your earthbound body is not limited to what earth can offer. You are living a translated existence, a boundless life.

"By faith Noah . . . built an ark" (v. 7). How did Noah decide to build an ark? Did he say to himself, *I'll bet God would be pleased if I just dropped everything and built an ark. You never know when an ark might come in handy.* No—God told Noah to build an ark. The story of Noah found in Genesis says over and over, "And Noah did all that the LORD commanded him" (Genesis 7:5). God calls this faith. God put a picture in Noah's mind of the promise that faith would bring into the earth (vv. 1–4), and Noah did all that the Lord commanded him. The picture that God painted for Noah, the promise with which He impregnated him, came to be on the earth on its due date. "In the six hundredth year of Noah's life, on the seventeenth day of the second month — on that day all the springs of the great deep burst forth, and the floodgates of the heavens were opened" (v. 11).

The author of Hebrews summarizes Abel, Enoch, and Noah. He is just getting warmed up. Then he moves to the patriarchs. The founding fathers. He puts more detail into these examples.

DAY 4

FAITH RELEASES THE POWER OF GOD

By faith Abraham, when called to go . . . obeyed and went" (Hebrews 11:8). Who initiated Abraham's journey? God called Abraham, Abraham obeyed, and God called it faith.

"The LORD had said to Abram, 'Go from your country, your people and your father's household to the land I will show you'" (Genesis 12:1). The Hebrew would be more accurately translated, "to the land I will [cause you to see]." The Lord paints a picture of the promise in Abraham's mind and then assured Abraham that God will cause him to see it. Abraham's response? "So Abram went, as the LORD had told him" (v. 4; author's emphasis). Fueled by faith.

"By faith he made his home in the promised land like a stranger in a foreign country; he lived in tents, as did Isaac and Jacob, who were heirs with him of the same promise. For he was looking forward to the city with foundations, whose architect and builder is God" (Hebrews 11:9–10).

Even though the circumstances of Abraham's life gave no evidence that the land was his, he knew that it was. Everybody else thought the land belonged to the Canaanites, but Abraham knew it belonged to him. He was content to live as if he were a stranger in a foreign country because he had the certainty of God's word. He was looking forward — the word means "to accept or to receive" — to the dwelling place God would design and build for him. There is no contextual reason to interpret this as looking for heaven. Rather, it clearly means that Abraham lived in his present circumstances, but was pregnant with the promise of God. God had promised him this very land in which he lived as his land and the land that would belong to his heirs. Looking from an eternal perspective, we know that ultimately that land is heaven, but in the real time experience of Abraham, he had been promised a land on planet earth. Even though his current situation looked from the earth as if he were a visitor in the land, in Abraham's mind he had conceived the promise and that was his reality. He kept his thoughts focused on the reality of the promise rather than the illusion of the momentary situation. Matthew Henry said, "Faith demonstrates to the eye of the mind the reality of those things which cannot be discerned by the eye of the body."

"By faith even Sarah herself received ability to conceive, even beyond the proper time of life, since she considered Him faithful who had promised. Therefore there was born even of one man, and him as good as dead at that, as many descendants as the stars of heaven in number, and innumerable as the sand which is by the seashore" (vv. 11–12 NASB).

(For this passage, I am switching to the New American Standard Bible because I am convinced this is a more accurate translation.) Sarah "received power"—the same word used for "received power" in Acts 1:8 (NASB). She was impregnated with the promise to become pregnant with a son. She received the power. She took what was offered to her. She was given the miraculous power to conceive "since" (because) she counted on God to deliver what He had promised. "Therefore" (as a result), the promise to Abraham, and by extension Sarah, took on substance and was manifested in the realm of earth. Fueled by faith, Sarah took possession of that which God offered to her and the picture God had painted in her mind showed up in the environment of earth.

The writer of Hebrews inserts a parenthetical thought here, in verses 13–16. He says that all these people were still in a faith position when they died, not having seen the fullness of the promises. God's promise to them would all find their fullness in Christ. These people only saw enough of the promise and experienced enough of its manifestation on earth to embrace its fullness from afar. When they died, they found the reality of what God was putting on the earth already fully formed in heaven. By means of their faith, God had been bringing what was in heaven into the environment of earth.

Then, the writer picks up where he had left off—with Abraham again. "By faith Abraham, when God tested him, offered Isaac as a sacrifice" (v. 17). I want to set verses 17–19 aside until the next section, where we will look carefully at them.

Moving to the next spotlighted life, we read, "By faith Isaac blessed Jacob and Esau in regard to their future" (v. 20). Isaac spoke his vision into the lives of his sons. He counted on the promise as his reality. In his blessing, Isaac was describing the picture God had painted in his mind as if it were certain and sure. He called what was not as though it were.

When Isaac blessed his sons, he was tricked by Jacob, the younger son, into pronouncing the blessing over Jacob that Isaac intended for the older son, Esau. When the trickery was discovered, Esau begged his father to bless him also. But here is how certain Isaac was about the reality of what he saw in his mind and pronounced in the form of blessing on Jacob. "Isaac answered Esau, 'I *have made him* lord over you and have made all his relatives his servants, and I *have sustained him* with grain and new wine. So what can I possibly do for you, my son?'" (Genesis 27:37; author's emphasis). Isaac considered the promise his reality.

"By faith Jacob, when he was dying, blessed each of Joseph's sons, and worshiped as he leaned on the top of his staff" (Hebrews 11:21). Jacob, Joseph's father, blessed Joseph's two oldest sons, announcing out loud over their lives the reality that he could see with his mind. Fueled by faith, he called what was not as though it were.

"By faith Joseph, when his end was near, spoke about the exodus of the Israelites from Egypt and gave instructions concerning the burial of his bones" (v. 22). Fueled by faith, as he was dying, Joseph spoke of the future events that God had shown him on the inside. At that time, Joseph's reputation was at its peak, and he would have been given a grand and elaborate burial in Egypt. At that time, the Israelites had not been enslaved and, in fact, were prospering and growing in Egypt. But Joseph could see with his heart that which could not be seen with the eyes. He demanded that his bones be brought to Canaan for burial when the time came and spoke the reality of the exodus of Israel long before it occurred on the earth. He believed what God's Word had shown him. He acted in accordance with that reality.

"By faith Moses' parents hid him for three months after he was born, because they saw he was no ordinary child, and they were not afraid of the king's edict" (v. 23). When Moses was born, God spoke a promise into the minds of his parents that had more influence over them than the king's edict. The vision that God implanted in them was the reality in which they acted, not the circumstances that tried to demand their attention. Fueled by faith, embracing the promise.

By faith Moses, when he had grown up, refused to be known as the son of Pharaoh's daughter. He chose to be mistreated along with the people of God rather than to enjoy the fleeting pleasures of sin. He regarded disgrace for the sake of Christ as of greater value than the treasures of Egypt, because he was looking ahead to his reward. By faith he left Egypt, not fearing the king's anger; he persevered because he saw him who is invisible. By faith he kept the Passover and the application of blood, so that the destroyer of the firstborn would not touch the firstborn of Israel (vv. 24–28).

By faith Moses responded to the call of God on his life and made decisions based on what he saw with spiritual vision rather than what he saw with his physical eyes. He kept on seeing "him who is invisible." That was the reality and the basis for all his actions. He lived according to the vision that God had placed in him. Fueled by faith.

"By faith the people passed through the Red Sea as on dry land" (v. 29). Moses led the children of Israel out of Egypt. Following God's voice, they found themselves in an impossible situation. As they were camped by the Red Sea, they looked up to see Pharaoh's army advancing toward them. Looking at the situation in the material realm, they saw no escape. Moses, however, wasn't looking at the material realm. "He persevered because he saw him who is invisible" (v. 27). Moses had spiritual vision.

Read Exodus 14:1–12. You will see that God was leading the Israelites into this seemingly impossible situation for a definite purpose: "I will gain glory for myself through Pharaoh and all his army, and the Egyptians will know that I am the LORD" (v. 4). God already had a plan. He knew what He wanted to do to save Israel. He had already planned to open the Red Sea and let Israel cross over on dry land. However, He didn't just do it. He said to Moses,

"Raise your staff and stretch out your hand over the sea to divide the water so the Israelites can go through the sea on dry ground." . . . Then Moses stretched out his hand over the sea, and all that night the LORD drove the sea back . . . and turned it into dry ground" (vv. 16, 21).

What drove the sea back and turned it into dry land? It was not Moses' staff. Moses' staff had no power. God drove the sea back. When Moses obeyed the present-tense voice of the Father. When he exercised faith, the power and provision of God showed up on the earth. Moses' faith-based obedience brought the fulfillment of the promise. The promise came by faith.

A similar incident occurred during Joshua's term of leadership. The story is found in Joshua 3. The Israelites needed to cross over the Jordan River. God said to Joshua: "Tell the priests who carry the ark of the covenant: 'When you reach the edge of the Jordan's waters, go and stand in the river'" (v. 8). What happened when they obeyed the present-tense voice of God? "Yet as soon as the priests who carried the ark reached the Jordan and their feet touched the water's edge, the water from upstream stopped flowing. It piled up in a heap a great distance away" (vv. 15–16). Faith released the power and provision of God. The promise came by faith.

"By faith the walls of Jericho fell, after the people had marched around them for seven days" (Hebrews 11:30). Consider the example of Joshua found in Joshua 6. As the Israelites were taking possession of the land God had given them, they needed to take the city of Jericho. Jericho was protected by a high and impenetrable wall. "Now the gates of Jericho were securely barred because of the Israelites. No one went out and no one came in" (v. 1). What would collapse the walls of Jericho? Military might? Physical strength? Clever strategy? Courage?

None of these things would do the job. It would take a mightier force than existed in the material realm. "By faith the walls of Jericho fell" (Hebrews 11:30). Nothing but faith would collapse the fortress around Jericho.

How did this wall-tumbling faith operate? "Then the LORD said to Joshua, 'See, I have delivered Jericho into your hands'" (Joshua 6:2). In the material realm, nothing had changed. Jericho's wall was just as strong as it had always been. The odds were against Israel — or so it appeared. Notice that God did not say, "I *will deliver* Jericho" but "I *have delivered* Jericho into your hands" (author's emphasis). God called what was not as though it were. Then He told Joshua exactly how to bring the victory out of heaven and establish it on the earth. You can read God's directives in verses 3–5. Joshua and the people did exactly as God had commanded. They were obedient to the present-tense voice of God. God called it faith, and it brought the promise. "By faith the walls of Jericho fell, after the army had marched around them for seven days" (Hebrews 11:30). Wall-tumbling faith is lived out in dynamic, active, bold obedience to God's voice.

"By faith the prostitute Rahab, because she welcomed the spies, was not killed with those who were disobedient" (v. 31). When Joshua was preparing the Israelites to take the city of Jericho, he sent two spies in to scout out the terrain. They were taken in by a woman named Rahab. Most English translations call her a prostitute, but the same word — both in Hebrew and the Greek word used here — is more often translated "innkeeper." If she was a prostitute, she was also an innkeeper, and she took in the two spies. The king of Jericho got wind of the spies' presence in Rahab's house, and he sent a command to her to produce them. She lied and said that she had turned them away. Then she crept up to the roof, where she had hidden them, and told them something that their eyes could not see.

Before the spies lay down for the night, she went up on the roof and said to them, "I know that the LORD has given you this land and that a great fear of you has fallen on us, so that all who live in this country are melting in fear because of you. We have heard how the LORD dried up the water of the Red Sea for you when you came out of Egypt, and what you did to Sihon and Og, the two kings of the Amorites east of the Jordan, whom you completely destroyed. When we heard of it, our hearts melted in fear and everyone's courage failed because of you, for the LORD your God is God in heaven above and on the earth below" (Joshua 2:8–11).

God had shown the inhabitants of the land that He had given the land to the Israelites. Rahab could see the truth, and she obeyed the truth. She lived in the reality of the truth. Everyone else was disobedient. Rahab's obedience to the reality that God had revealed to her resulted in her salvation and the salvation of her family. Fueled by faith, she lined herself up with God's promise and the promise came by faith.

The definition remains consistent. God calls things that are not as though they were. He talks about the eternal truth, not the appearance of the moment. God does not direct your attention to the need but to the supply. Before a need enters your experience, God has fully prepared the supply. Your faith will get the finished work of God out of heaven and onto earth.

What are the circumstances in your life that look overwhelming and impossible?

Now place those circumstances against the backdrop of the amazing power and astonishing love of God. Do they look different now? Do you see them as they are?

God is spotlighting your life right now, holding you out as proof to those around you. Describe situations in your life right now that are forcing faith into the open.

Every circumstance, every need, every desire is God's entry point into your life. Every difficulty is simply highlighting the exact place where God will apply His power. Every challenge or obstacle is God's opportunity to substantiate His promises. Problems are nothing more than labor pains as God brings about the birth of His vision.

The truth is this: every mountain becomes a road. Every desert abounds with streams and pools of water. Lush gardens grow in the wastelands. Treasures are hidden in the darkness.

In each case, God initiated the call and the faith hero responded in obedience to God's present-tense voice. In every case, the obedience provided God the opportunity to show His power on earth.

The promises of God come from the spiritual end of the continuum of reality, heaven, to the material end of the continuum, earth, by the exercise of faith. When you live by faith — a life marked by obedience — then the vision inside you will begin to take on substance in the material realm.

The adversity in your life right now is essential for preparing you for God's vision. Let adversity do its intended work.

DAY 5

FAITH IN ITS FINISHED FORM

"Looking unto Jesus the author and finisher of our faith" (Hebrews 12:2 KJV).

Faith in its finished form results in the power and provision of God manifested in the circumstances of earth. The perfecting and finishing of our faith is accomplished through difficulties and challenges of life.

As we face challenges, it trains us in the ways of faith, it trains us to keep our focus on the reality instead of the shadow, and it removes all the flesh out of the vision God has given us. Like muscles in the physical body, faith grows by resistance training—by being forced to do heavy lifting.

Consider it pure joy, my brothers and sisters, whenever you face trials of many kinds, because you know that the testing of your faith produces perseverance. Let perseverance finish its work so that you may be mature and complete, not lacking anything (James 1:2–4).

Difficulty becomes blessing. Trials become joy. As William Shakespeare wrote in his play, *As You Like It,* "Sweet are the uses of adversity."

CIRCUMCISING THE VISION

When God impregnates you with promise and makes vision grow in you, that vision is designed and tailored to fit you and only you. It fits you exactly. When God describes His will, He uses three words: "good, pleasing, and perfect" (Romans 12:2). The word *perfect* means "a perfect fit." His will for you is beneficial to you ("good"); it will bring you pleasure and will please you ("pleasing"); and it will fit you to down to the last detail ("perfect"). You love the vision. You're supposed to. During the gestation period, as you move toward the fulfillment of the good, pleasing, perfect vision, there are times that seem less than good, perfect, or pleasing. But in the end, you were designed to host just this vision and it will fit you.

As the vision develops, the time comes when you are forced to recognize that although the vision is God's, it has some of your flesh wrapped around it. When I say "flesh," I am talking about those parts of your life that are still fueled by your human nature. Your flesh wants to own and control and possess and manage and manipulate. God is always working in you to free you of your flesh and move you more and more into the power of the Spirit. To that end, He arranges crisis moments at which you are brought face-to-face with your flesh and the claim it is trying to have on God's vision. Those times are painful, but they are the most productive times of all.

Let's go back to our review of Hebrews 11 and Abraham, called to offer Isaac on the altar.

ABRAHAM

Earlier, we looked at Abraham's faith described in the Book of Hebrews. To see this principle of circumcising the vision, we need to look at the account in the Book of Genesis and then the commentary on the story in the Book of Hebrews. (I developed this concept in my book *Altar'd* as a principle of how to put our flesh on the Cross. The principle also clearly applies to our concept of the vision with which God has impregnated us.)

The story begins,

God tested Abraham. He said to him, "Abraham!" "Here I am," he replied. Then God said, "Take your son, your only son, whom you love — Isaac — and go to the region of Moriah. Sacrifice him there as a burnt offering on a mountain I will show you." Early the next morning Abraham got up and loaded his donkey (Genesis 22:1–3).

God tested Abraham. The word *test* is better translated "proved." When God tests, He is not trying to discover what is inside us. He knows what is inside us. He is *proving* what is inside us. He is bringing what is inside to the outside. Don't think of this as a trick on God's part. He is not trying to trip up Abraham; He is proving to Abraham what God knows is in him. He is using this crisis moment to free Abraham of his flesh. In the Book of Hebrews, we have an explanation of God's dealing with Abraham.

By faith Abraham, when God tested him, offered Isaac as a sacrifice. He who had embraced the promises was about to sacrifice his one and only son, even though God had said to him, "It is through Isaac that your offspring will be reckoned." Abraham reasoned that God could raise the dead, and so in a manner of speaking he did receive Isaac back from death." (Hebrews 11:17–19)

You remember the story. Just as Abraham was about to plunge the knife into Isaac, the Lord stopped him. Yet the writer of Hebrews says, "Abraham . . . offered Isaac." He uses a verb tense that indicates a completed action. Didn't Abraham stop short of completing the offering? Yet the Bible says that he offered Isaac, completing the sacrifice. When did Abraham complete the offering of Isaac?

Go back to the account in Genesis 22. In this abbreviated account we read that God called Abraham to offer Isaac as a sacrifice, and the next morning Abraham got up and saddled his donkey for the trip. But between God's call and Abraham's obedience lay a long, dark night of struggle. You and I are left to imagine how intense that struggle must have been. We can guess at the agony through which Abraham passed. Our hearts hear Abraham crying out something that reminds of Jesus' struggle in the garden of Gethsemane: "My Father, if it possible, may this cup be taken from me" (Matthew 26:39). And before the morning broke, we hear him just as clearly say, "Yet, not as I will, but as you will." It was in that dark night that Abraham completed the offering of Isaac. It was there that God received what He was asking for. How do I know that?

One of the layers of meaning in this account is that it is a picture of the Crucifixion. Follow the timeline with me. Abraham got up, saddled his donkey, and set out for the place God would show Him (Genesis 22:2). He traveled for *three days* (v. 4) then took Isaac to the top of the mountain and prepared to sacrifice him on the altar. Instead of killing Isaac, God stopped him and Abraham received Isaac back in a resurrection: "And so in a manner of speaking he did receive Isaac back from death" (Hebrews 11:19). If Abraham traveled for three days and on the third day received Isaac back in a type of resurrection, then when did Isaac die? The sacrifice was completed on the long, agonizing night that brought about Abraham's yielded obedience. Three days later, Abraham received Isaac back in a type of resurrection.

God considered the sacrifice to be completed. God got what He was after. What did God want from Abraham? What was the sacrifice?

Abraham was connected to Isaac in two ways: First, Isaac was the son of his flesh. He was to Abraham "your son, your only son, whom you love — Isaac" (Genesis 22:2). You can imagine how very strong that connection was. After having waited and yearned for this son until all rational hope was gone and his and Sarah's bodies were long past childbearing years, at last Isaac was born. As his son, in the days of Abraham, Isaac was his property. He had the right to do with him as he chose. You know that every choice Abraham made concerning Isaac was made out of an overflow of love.

Abraham was connected to Isaac in another way. Isaac was also the child of promise, born by the power of the Spirit (Galatians 4:28–29). It was through Isaac that all of the promise of God — that which had defined Abraham's entire adult life — was to be realized. "He who had received the promises was about to sacrifice his one and only son, *even though God had said* to him, 'It is through Isaac that your offspring will be reckoned'" (Hebrews 11:17–19; author's emphasis). Abraham was connected to Isaac spiritually. Isaac was to Abraham both the child of his flesh and the child of the promise.

On the night that Abraham completed the offering, Isaac did not die to Abraham, but Abraham died to his flesh connection with Isaac. He let his father flesh die. He relinquished ownership. That was the night he laid Isaac on the altar. It was Abraham's crucifixion, not Isaac's.

In requiring Abraham to die to his flesh connection, God did not require Abraham to die to the spiritual promise. Abraham, I believe, was more alive than ever to the promise in Isaac. As he reached the place of the sacrifice, "He said to his servants, 'Stay here with the donkey while I and the boy go over there. *We will worship* and then *we will come back to you*'" (Genesis 22:5; author's emphasis). The writer of Hebrews says, "Abraham reasoned that God could even raise the dead, and so in a manner of speaking he did receive Isaac back from death" (Hebrews 11:19). By the time he had become fully yielded to the voice of God, by the time he had dealt the deathblow to his own flesh, he had reached a new level of faith in God. He was absolutely certain that, no matter what path the promise took, the promise of God would not fail.

Do you have an Isaac on the altar?

How does your heart respond to the circumcision of your flesh right now?

The promise of prayer is a heart so transformed and so tenderized to the movement of God in your life that you learn the kind of obedience that is the vehicle that brings the power of God from heaven to earth.

WEEK 4
THE PRACTICE OF PRAYER

The pursuit of any goal requires a narrowed focus. Choosing to live a praying life — a life through which the power of God is free to flow — involves sacrifice. In this, it is no different from any other rock-solid commitment. Whatever you choose to pursue will mean that you sacrifice something else. The key is this: If the goal is sufficiently attractive, the sacrifice required will be irrelevant. In fact, the more focused on your goal you are, the less you will perceive the requirements as "sacrifices." . . .

What you have to give up in order to reach your goal will feel more like being freed of weights. "Let us throw off everything that hinders and the sin that so easily entangles. And let us run with perseverance the race marked out for us" *(Hebrews 12:1). What we once considered gain we now see as loss. What we once counted as treasure we now know is rubbish. But whatever was to my profit I now consider loss for the sake of Christ* (Philippians 3:7– 8; paraphrase).

— Live a Praying Life®: Open Your Life to God's Power and Provision

DAY I

et me suggest some practical ways to pray through adversity. First,
join a prayer group. You will find so many advantages to praying with
others in a small-group setting. For example:

1. You won't be bearing your burden alone. You'll have others who can
   pick up the slack when you feel bereft of faith. You will have a group
   that won't get tired of your request as you need prayer over and over.
   You have a group whom the Lord will remind and call to prayer for
   you at strategic times.

2. You will have the experience of the Holy Spirit flowing among you
   and awakening thoughts and confirming His work.

3. You will become part of other people's burdens, which will help you
   keep from praying obsessively (worrying, actually) about your own
   adversity all the time. You will get to see God at work in other lives,
   and that will strengthen your faith.

4. You will have a place where you can be raw and honest and where
   you will know your confidences are respected.

Second, don't make your adversity the only content of prayer. Even
while your adversity is in high gear, the Lord will be working in many
areas of your life. As you see Him working—and hear His voice—in
other areas, it will feed your faith.

Third, don't let the enemy turn any part of your experience into
an opportunity to bring condemnation. You will have emotions and
reactions and moments that you know are fueled by your flesh. You
don't have to feel condemned. Just acknowledge: *That's my flesh. I
know it's there. But I'm not going to let it rule me.*

Fourth, recognize the enemy's lies, and reject them for the truth. The
enemy's strategy is to exchange truth for lies (Romans 1:25), so reverse
his strategy and exchange lies for truth. Some of his best lies in times

of extended adversity are: (1) You don't deserve God's intervention. (2) You don't have enough faith. (3) God helps other people, but He doesn't help you. You must not be one of the favorites. (4) It's hopeless. It's too late. It's too far gone.

Fifth, when worry or concern enters your thoughts, let your visual brain see the reality of Jesus there with your loved one, or in the future where your fear is directed, or present in the situation that concerns you. This is not an attempt to visualize an outcome but to see the truth. Jesus is present in power and authority wherever your worry is.

What lies have gained traction in your life through your adversity? What is the truth those lies are trying to obscure?

DAY 2

This last week, we're changing the rhythm. You have worked through some tangled emotions and waded in some deep waters. Use Days 2 through 4 to go back and review what the Lord has spoken to you in your adversity. Let the Lord distill the main message to your heart from each week. What truth changed the way you are living a praying life in adversity?

What is the main takeaway from Week 1 for your life? Write out your summation of what the Lord spoke to you.

DAY 3

What is the main takeaway from Week 2 for your life? Write out your summation of what the Lord spoke to you.

DAY 4

What is the main takeaway from Week 3 for your life? Write out your summation of what the Lord spoke to you.

DAY 5

GIVE GOD A YEAR

Let God use your adversity to draw you ever closer to Him on every front. Sometimes the adversity makes us listless and sucks the joy and energy from our times of prayer.

I invite you now on a 52-week odyssey of praying and opening your life to God's voice and to His present-tense, at-hand power. One of the challenges about the discipline of praying is the tendency to fall into a rut. In the following pages, I suggest 52 ways of praying actively. Maybe your family would like to take this journey together, or your prayer group, or your church. Meet together weekly to discuss and share the week's experience and encourage one another and join your voices in agreement with the Word of God. Happy traveling!

52 PRAYER POINTS

1.

"In the LORD's hand the king's heart is a stream of water that he channels toward all who please him" (Proverbs 21:1).

If your thoughts wander during your prayertime, instead of trying to force them back into your preset agenda, try following them. Perhaps the Lord has another agenda.

2.

"But when you pray, go into your room, close the door and pray to your Father, who is unseen" (Matthew 6:6).

Set a time for daily prayer. Consider it an unbreakable commitment. Keep your set appointment every day for one week. For one solid week, let your scheduled prayertime be the centerpiece of your day. Arrange everything else to fit around it.

3.

"Very early in the morning, while it was still dark, Jesus got up, left the house and went off to a solitary place, where he prayed" (Mark 1:35).

Give God the firstfruits of your day. For one week, give the very first 30 minutes of your day to prayer.

4.

"But Jesus often withdrew to lonely places and prayed" (Luke 5:16).

Find a place in your home where you can be alone and undistracted during your prayertime. Keep your Bible, prayer journal, pen, and whatever tools you use in that place so that everything is ready. During your prayertime each day, this is a sacred place.

5.

"I saw the Lord, high and exalted, seated on a throne; and the train of his robe filled the temple" (Isaiah 6:1).

As you start your prayertime—before you say anything—let your mind's eye see Him, high and exalted, and yourself in a position of worship before Him. Inwardly, stay in that posture until His glory fills your thoughts as the train of His robe fills the temple.

6.

"But Jesus said, 'Someone touched me; I know that power has gone out from me'" (Luke 8:46).

Take time to become truly alive to His presence with you. Be aware that as you touch Him through prayer, His power is released into your life.

7.

"My people, hear my teaching; listen to the words of my mouth" (Psalm 78:1).

Read your Bible this morning with the awareness that you are listening to the words of His mouth. Stop at the first word, phrase, or thought that captures your attention, and let the Father speak to you about it. Let it shape your prayers.

8.

"We are the clay, you are the potter; we are all the work of your hand" (Isaiah 64:8).

This week, practice the prayer of pliability. Instead of focusing on what you want God to do for you, focus on allowing Him to shape your desires until they match His. Accept each situation in your life as His hand shaping your thoughts, character, and longings.

9.

"Not my will, but yours be done" (Luke 22:42).

This week, let these words be the only prayer you pray about situations that confront you. Focus on relinquishing every situation to Him to be a platform for His power.

10.

"I will remember the deeds of the LORD" (Psalm 77:11).

This week, try writing out your prayers. It will help you stay focused and will create a record of God's work in your life.

11.

"My tongue will proclaim your righteousness, your praises all day long" (Psalm 35:28).

This week, practice praying out loud during your private prayertime. It will make your prayer experience more concrete and will help you keep your mind focused.

12.

"Fix these words of mine in your hearts and minds . . . talking about them when you sit at home and when you walk along the road, when you lie down and when you get up" (Deuteronomy 11:18–19).

This week, try walking as you pray. Walk through your neighborhood or around your yard. You will be more able to keep your mind open to new thoughts the Lord might introduce. You are likely to find yourself spending more time with Him.

13.

"I have strayed like a lost sheep. Seek your servant, for I have not forgotten your commands" (Psalm 119:176).

Between you and the Lord, settle on a phrase that He can remind you of throughout the day to call you back into intimacy when you have turned your heart outward. Find a phrase like *Only You.* Something short and simple that can be a shorthand prayer that speaks volumes.

14.

"I thank my God every time I remember you" (Philippians 1:3).

This week, practice using "prayer triggers." Let even fleeting thoughts of your friends, loved ones, and "enemies" turn into prayer for them. The prayer can be as simple as breathing the name, "Jesus."

15.

"I will sing the LORD's praise, for he has been good to me" (Psalm 13:6).

This week, during your prayertime, sing to the Lord. Use a hymnal or songbook; sing songs you have memorized; sing the Scriptures to your own tunes; make up songs. Sing out loud or sing inwardly.

16.

"I spread out my hands to you; I thirst for you like a parched land" (Psalm 143:6).

This week, during your prayertime, use different worship postures: kneel, lift your hands, or fall on your face before Him. You may do this outwardly, or inwardly — in the inner sanctuary of your own soul.

17.

"Praise be to the Lord, to God our Savior, who daily bears our burdens" (Psalm 68:19).

In your prayer journal, list the following headings: (1) anxieties, (2) responsibilities, (3) needs, and (4) desires. Under each, list everything that comes to mind. As you write each thought down, consider it an act of surrender. You are handing each thing over to Him. Do this every day for a week. You will most likely be repeating some things every day. That's fine. He *"daily* bears our burdens"* (author's emphasis).

18.

"Here I am! I stand at the door and knock. If anyone hears my voice and opens the door, I will come in and eat with that person, and they with me" (Revelation 3:20).

Prayer is opening your life to Jesus. He is at the door, knocking. In prayer, you are simply responding to His love that seeks you out. Times of prayer are times of fellowship with Him, as if He were in your home sharing a meal with you. This week, during your prayertime, let your mind's eye see Him as He sits just across from you. Talk right to Him and let Him talk to you.

19.

"But seek his kingdom, and these things will be given to you as well" (Luke 12:31).

Your daily prayertime lays the groundwork for an ongoing awareness of His presence. This week, during your prayertime, ask Him to alert you and call your attention to kingdom moments throughout your day. Watch for opportunities to enjoy fellowship with Him—waiting in lines, performing mundane tasks, for example. Being consciously aware of His presence will transform life's irritants into opportunities for fellowship with Him.

20.

"Speak, for your servant is listening" (1 Samuel 3:10).

The most important prayer skill is learning to listen to the Living Voice. This week, let listening to Him be the main focus of your prayertime. Let 1 Samuel 3:10 be your only request. Listen for Him in His Word, in the quietness of your heart, in the circumstances of your day, in fresh ideas that come to mind, in new understanding that settles on you. Learn to listen. Write down what you think you sense Him saying to you.

21.

"Do not be anxious about anything, but in every situation, by prayer and petition, with thanksgiving, present your requests to God. And the peace of God, which transcends all understanding, will guard your hearts and your minds in Christ Jesus" (Philippians 4:6–7).

What situations are causing you anxiety? Write them down. Big and little. Major and minor. Now, go back through your list and practice offering the sacrifice of thanksgiving as an act of obedience. First, thank God for allowing the circumstance in your life because you trust Him to bring about a good and beneficial outcome from it. Then, let the Spirit bring to your mind things that you can be thankful about in that circumstance—ways that you already see God's hand.

22.

"Don't you know that you yourselves are God's temple and that God's Spirit dwells in your midst?" (1 Corinthians 3:16).

You are God's dwelling place. He is at home in you. Focus on that reality this morning. You do not have to seek Him out and get His attention — He has sought you out. In the Old Testament, worship in the temple engaged all the senses. This week, create an atmosphere for your prayertime that engages your senses. Light a fragrant candle. Play worshipful music. Let your senses enter into the experience of worship.

23.

"He wakens me morning by morning, wakens my ear to listen like one being instructed" (Isaiah 50:4).

This week, during your prayertime, consider that you are there at His invitation. He has invited you to spend time alone with Him because He has something beneficial to teach you and say to you. Consider how that changes the atmosphere of your prayertime. Write your observations in your journal.

24.

"As a bridegroom rejoices over his bride, so will your God rejoice over you" (Isaiah 62:5).

This week, begin your prayertime by feeling the Lord's pleasure in your presence. Be aware of how delighted He is to have time alone with you. Let His love for you and His joy in you fill your soul with peace and contentment.

25.

"Whoever obeys his command will come to no harm, and the wise heart will know the proper time and procedure" (Ecclesiastes 8:5).

During your prayertimes this week, ask the Lord to tell you anything He wants you to do today — any action He wants you to take. Express your faith to Him that, when the time comes, you will know what to do and how to do it. Be alert every moment of your day for His command.

26.

"You have searched me, LORD, and you know me" (Psalm 139:1).

Each morning this week, during your prayertime, use Psalm 139:1–6. Read it through slowly each morning, concentrating on each phrase. Focus on a different verse each morning, turning it into your personal prayer and allowing the Spirit of God to speak personally to you. Keep that verse in your thoughts all day long, praying it as situations arise.

27.

"Be still, and know that I am God" (Psalm 46:10).

This week during your prayertimes, focus on being in the moment. Let these words wrap themselves around your heart: "Be still, and know that I am God." Let the power of His presence flood you, filling you with confidence, peace, boldness. When He says, "I am God," what is He saying to you? Each morning, write down what it means to you that He is God.

28.

"Search me, God, and know my heart; test me and know my anxious thoughts. See if there is any offensive way in me, and lead me in the way everlasting" (Psalm 139:23–24).

This week, open your life to the Father so that He can clean out the clutter. Let Him bring to light anything that is keeping you from experiencing all that He has to offer. Don't resist Him. He wants your life to be filled with His abundance and wants to rid you of anything that dilutes His power in you. Write down what He brings to mind.

29.

"This is the day which the LORD has made; let us rejoice and be glad in it" (Psalm 118:24 NASB).

This week, let this be your first thought every morning: *This is the day the Lord has appointed for you. He has given you this day.* Embrace everything He brings into this day. When it brings difficulty or disappointment, think of your circumstance as a faith lab. Every little joy or pleasure it brings is a gift from the Father. Start your prayertimes this week by settling this in your mind: I will rejoice and be glad in *this* day.

30.

"Let this be written for a future generation, that a people not yet created may praise the LORD" (Psalm 102:18)

This week, during your prayertimes, compose a letter to future generations. Write a paragraph or a sentence or a thought each day. What do you want to pass along to those who will come after you? What do you want to leave them as a spiritual legacy? This will help you focus on what God means to you and will stir up genuine praise and worship.

31.

"Those who know your name will trust in you, for you, LORD, have never forsaken those who seek you" (Psalm 9:10).

This week, each morning focus on a name for Christ. Think through what that name says to you in your present circumstance. What promise does His name hold? As you pray, let Him show you each need or desire in light of His name — who He is. Use these names: (1) *Refiner,* Malachi 3:3; (2) *God with Us,* Matthew 1:23; (3) *the Light,* John 1:9; (4) *Bread of life,* John 6:35; (5) *Good Shepherd,* John 10:11; (6) *Teacher and Lord,* John 13:13; (7) *Vine,* John 15:5.

32.

"I keep my eyes always on the LORD. With him at my right hand, I will not be shaken. Therefore my heart is glad and my tongue rejoices; my body also will rest secure" (Psalm 16:8–9).

Let the peace in your innermost being spill over into your body. This week, during your prayertimes, start each morning by consciously relaxing. Breathe in deeply, then breathe out slowly. As you breathe out, let your inner peace fill your body. Feel your muscles relaxing. Enjoy the feeling of complete peace and restfulness. Let thoughts of Him flood your mind and permeate your body with peace.

33.

"Our Father in heaven, hallowed be your name" (Matthew 6:9).

Begin to pray through the Lord's Prayer, letting each phrase take root in your heart and grow fruit. This week, focus each morning on Matthew 6:9. Consider God's role as Father. What does that mean in the context of your needs and desires? Write out your thoughts in your prayer journal. How can His name be exalted and hallowed in the midst of your needs? Write out your thoughts.

34.

"Your kingdom come, your will be done, on earth as it is in heaven" (Matthew 6:10).

This week, focus on Matthew 6:10 each morning. Bring each situation to the Lord and pray, "Let Your will be done in this in every detail. Let Your kingdom rule take effect in this in every detail." Bring every detail of your situations before Him, asking Him to take full charge.

35.

"Give us today our daily bread" (Matthew 6:11).

This week, focus on Matthew 6:11 each morning. Ask Him for His provision in every circumstance and every need the day presents. Rest in His willingness and His ability to meet every need as it arises.

36.

"Forgive us our debts, as we also have forgiven our debtors" (Matthew 6:12).

This week, focus on Matthew 6:12. Let the Father lead you in identifying and forgiving those who have hurt or offended you. Let Him set you free from the burden of bitterness.

37.

"And lead us not into temptation, but deliver us from the evil one" (Matthew 6:13).

This week, focus on Matthew 6:13. Daily, ask the Lord to lead you in paths that will help you avoid temptation. Listen to Him as He brings thoughts to your mind about how to avoid placing yourself in temptation's path. Obey.

38.

"That your ways may be known on earth, your salvation among all nations" (Psalm 67:2).

This week, use your newspaper or newsmagazine as a prayer guide. Find a current situation that engages your interest. Avoid the tendency to pray your political agenda. Instead, pray that every aspect of the situation will be God's tool for bringing about the right outcome for the big picture. Pray for every Christian who might be involved or affected. Pray for every nonbeliever. Pray for every detail you read about. The media members who are reporting it. The leaders who are making decisions. Pray that it will all work together to bring glory to His name.

39.

"Carry each other's burdens, and in this way you will fulfill the law of Christ" (Galatians 6:1–3).

This week, ask the Lord to place on your mind someone for whom you are to pray. It may be someone you know well, or it may be someone with whom you are only acquainted. It may even be someone you only know of. Write the name down. Be faithful in praying each time the name comes to your remembrance. Watch for the amazing ways the Lord will lead you in prayer and the ways He will give you glimpses of His work. Write them in your journal.

40.

"I have learned the secret of being content in any and every situation" (Philippians 4:12).

In which areas of your life do you lack contentment? Write them down as they come to mind. Are you looking to some external circumstance or some other person for contentment? This week, focus your prayertime on asking the Lord to create in you a heart that rests contentedly in Him and His plans for you.

41.

"I urge you, brothers and sisters, by our Lord Jesus Christ and by the love of the Spirit, to join me in my struggle by praying to God for me" (Romans 15:30).

This week, ask someone else to pray for you in your struggles. Let the Lord guide you to the right person. During your prayertimes, when your struggle comes to mind, rest in the fact that someone else is carrying that burden for you this week.

42.

"When you fast, do not look somber as the hypocrites do, for they disfigure their faces to show others they are fasting. Truly I tell you, they have received their reward in full. But when you fast, put oil on your head and wash your face, so that it will not be obvious to men that you are fasting, but only to your Father, who is unseen; and your Father, who sees what is done in secret, will reward you" (Matthew 6:16–18).

This week, plan to fast one meal per day. Replace that meal with concentrated time in the Word of God and prayer. Let any hunger you experience serve as a call to prayer. Ask the Lord to give you as intense a craving for Him as your body has for food. Record your experience in your prayer journal each morning.

43.

"He blesses the home of the righteous" (Proverbs 3:33).

This week, have your time of prayer in a different room in your home each morning. Focus your prayertime around the aspect of your life or your family's life that room represents to you. Let the Spirit bring ideas to mind.

44.

"I will walk in my house with a blameless heart" (Psalm 101:2).

This week, focus your prayertime on your relationship with each member of your family, or those who are like family to you. Each morning, concentrate on one person. Pray for God's purpose to be established in that relationship. Ask Him to show you any ways that your heart is not blameless in your own home.

45.

"The word is very near you; it is in your mouth and in your heart so you may obey it" (Deuteronomy 30:14).

This week, during your prayertimes, read the Scripture out loud. You will find that your mind stays focused better and that hearing the words and speaking them brings out nuances that you have missed by reading silently.

46.

"Therefore encourage one another and build each other up, just as in fact you are doing" (1 Thessalonians 5:11).

This week, prepare for your daily prayertime by gathering note cards or stationery of some sort. Ask the Lord to place on your heart someone who needs encouragement. During your prayertime, write out your prayer for that person and mail it to him or her. Pray for and encourage someone different each morning.

47.

"We always thank God for all of you and continually mention you in our prayers. We continually remember before our God and Father your work produced by faith, your labor prompted by love, and your endurance inspired by hope in our Lord Jesus Christ" (1 Thessalonians 1:2–3).

This week, keep your stationery handy. During your prayertimes, let the Spirit remind you of people who have been instrumental in your spiritual formation. As you are thanking God for them, write notes of appreciation to them. Some may be currently in your life. Some may be from years before. Rejoice in the treasure God has put in your life in the form of His people.

48.

"Finally, be strong in the Lord and in his mighty power. Put on the full armor of God, so that you can take your stand against the devil's

schemes. . . . And pray in the Spirit on all occasions with all kinds of prayers and requests. With this in mind, be alert and always keep on praying for all the Lord's people" (Ephesians 6:10–11, 18).

This week, pray through the spiritual armor that Paul describes in Ephesians 6:10–11. Each morning, read the entire passage, expecting the Spirit to make it fresh for you. Then, each day focus on one piece of armor. Let the Lord speak to you about it as you spiritually "put on": (1) belt of truth; (2) breastplate of righteousness; (3) shoes of the gospel of peace; (4) shield of faith; (5) helmet of salvation; (6) sword of the Spirit. On the seventh day, read verse 18 carefully. Once armed, how do you take your stand against the devil's schemes? Through prayer.

49.

"Many are the plans in a person's heart, but it is the LORD's purpose that prevails" (Proverbs 19:21).

This week, focus your prayertime on embracing the Lord's purpose in your every action, every plan, every endeavor. Each morning, list your plans for the day. Yield them to God's purposes. Be ready to change them if the Lord should direct you to. Be alert for how God is working out His long-term purposes through your short-term plans.

50.

"Fixing our eyes on Jesus, the pioneer and perfecter of our faith" (Hebrews 12:2).

This week, be fully aware of Jesus. He is God's everything. During your daily prayertime, before you do anything else, fix your inner eyes on Jesus. As you go through your day, let your inner eyes see Jesus present in every situation. When you think of a friend or a family member, let your inner eyes see Jesus there with that person.

51.

"I instruct you in the way of wisdom and lead you along straight paths. When you walk, your steps will not be hampered; when you run, you will not stumble" (Proverbs 4:11–12).

This week, turn this promise into a prayer. Memorize these verses or write them out and take them with you. Pray this promise as you make every decision — big or little, business or personal. Record your experiences in your prayer journal.

52.

"I pray that the eyes of your heart may be enlightened in order that you may know the hope to which he has called you" (Ephesians 1:18).

This week, plan a prayer excursion. Go by yourself, enlist a fellow intercessor, or go as a prayer group. Go to a public place — a mall, a restaurant, a ball game. Pray flash prayers for people you encounter. Ask God to open the eyes of their hearts so that they will know the hope to which He has called them. If you are with a partner or a group, you may wish to pray out loud in conversational tones. You do not need to close your eyes to pray.

New Hope® Publishers is a division of WMU®, an international organization that challenges Christian believers to understand and be radically involved in God's mission. For more information about WMU, go to wmu.com. More information about New Hope books may be found at NewHopeDigital.com. New Hope books may be purchased at your local bookstore.

Use the QR reader on your
smartphone to visit us online at
NewHopeDigital.com

If you've been blessed by this book, we would like to hear your story. The publisher and author welcome your comments and suggestions at: newhopereader@wmu.org.

Take Your Faith Journey One Step Further with New Hope Interactive Bible Studies!

Bible study made engaging, convenient, and interactive. Visit NewHopeInteractive.com

MEDIA

NEWS TV RADIO INTERNET SHOW PEOPLE INTERESTS TODAY

For information about our books and authors, visit NewHopeDigital.com. Experience sample chapters, podcasts, author interviews and more! Download the New Hope app for your iPad, iPhone, or Android!